Page 43

GOD'S LAYERED LOVE

© 2014 by Al Houghton. All rights reserved. This book is protected under the copyright laws of the United States of America. No part of this publication may be reproduced, stored on a retrieval system, or transmitted in any way by any means – electronic, mechanical, photocopy, recording, or otherwise – without the express permission of the copyright holder.

Author's note: Capitalization of certain words are for emphasis only.

All scripture quotations, not otherwise indicated, are from *The New King James Version*, © 1982 by Thomas Nelson, Inc. Used by permission.

Reproduction of cover or text in whole or in part without the express written consent of the author is unlawful according to the 1976 United States Copyright Act.

Printed in the United States of America

Published by
Word At Work Ministries, Inc.
P.O. Box 366 ♦ Placentia, California 92871 ♦ U.S.A.

www.wordatwork.org

ISBN 978-0-940252-03-5

GOD'S LAYERED LOVE

AL HOUGHTON

Table of Contents

Acknowledgements	7
Introduction	11
1. God's Layered Love, An Overview	15
2. Layer One - Evangelistic Love	23
3. Layer Two - Pastoral Love	33
4. The Eternal Purpose of Forbearance	47
5. Layer Three - Prophetic Love	57
6. Layer Four - Teaching Love	73
7. Forgiveness - The Key to Affliction	81
8. Affliction - Key to Executing the Anointing to Spoil	97
9. Layer Five - Apostolic Love	113
10. Apostolic Love in Judges	133
11. The Power to Resist	143
12. Understanding Judicial Love	153
13. Why does Love Terminate?	161
14. Love Executes Justice	179
15. The Love that Saves, Also Cuts Off	185
16. Love Never Fails	191
17. Love in its Fullness	217

Acknowledgements

Foremost, I wish to thank my wife Jayne who for years has diligently lived the truth of God's love by word and deed. Jayne has tirelessly continued to help my eyes open to the subtleties of God's Love in justice and judgment. I cannot honorably present this subject without crediting her with the decades of spiritual growth necessary for me to truly present the width and breadth of both the Priestly and Kingly Christ.

Many thanks to Paul Flotho, who watered the seed that grew into this book! Love is a subject with which the majority of believers are most familiar but the Judicial side of that love is largely obscured. I have known and appreciated Paul and his wife Mary since their giant step of faith right after our graduation from seminary and ordination into ministry. Paul built a plywood camper for a Toyota Pickup and left Anaheim, California for Mexico as a missionary with no promise of support from anyone. His faith humbled me. He spent many years as a missionary to Mexico and Spanish-speaking countries, developed a radio ministry and published books while raising three girls all by faith!

Steve Hake provided the organizational suggestions responsible for chapter presentations, thereby adding needed clarity. Tom Pillsbury provided a number of technical editorial inputs which greatly enhanced the manuscript. Additional pastoral suggestions by Gary and Linda Hall,

Jerry Ashley, George and Linda Duarte, Larry Brewer and A.J. Getz proved invaluable in completing this manuscript. And my acknowledgements would not be complete without a special thanks to my daughter, Julie Houghton, who tirelessly shepherded this project through to completion.

I have the great joy of knowing a select group of people who share a likeness with those mentioned in Hebrews 11:32-38,

> *And what more shall I say? For the time would fail me to tell of Gideon and Barak and Samson and Jephthah, also of David and Samuel and the prophets: who through faith subdued kingdoms, worked righteousness, obtained promises, stopped the mouths of lions, quenched the violence of fire, escaped the edge of the sword, out of weakness were made strong, became valiant in battle, turned to flight the armies of the aliens. Women received their dead raised to life again. Others were tortured, not accepting deliverance, that they might obtain a better resurrection. Still others had trial of mockings and scourgings, yes, and of chains and imprisonment. They were stoned, they were sawn in two, were tempted, were slain with the sword. They wandered about in sheepskins and goatskins, being destitute, afflicted, tormented – of whom the world was not worthy. They wandered in deserts and mountains, in dens and caves of the earth.*

There are Christians today of whom the world is not worthy. Since the seed that grew to become this book was planted and watered by two such people, *God's Layered Love* is also dedicated to all the believers who will qualify as pillars of righteousness *"of whom the world is not worthy."*

◆ God's Layered Love ◆

> These are at no charge and come once a month (ck no for offering envelope)
> (Can get online free)

Introduction

Love is the deepest subject in the Bible and possibly the most misunderstood. In Acts 2:36 Peter explained Pentecost, *"Therefore let all the house of Israel know assuredly that God has made this Jesus, whom you crucified, both Lord and Christ."* *"Lord"* is the Greek word **koo-ree-os**, Judge of all the Earth, and *"Christ"* is **khris-tos**, Savior of all the Earth! **Khris-tos** love "turns-the-other-cheek" while **koo-ree-os** love employs a "Rod of Iron" when needed and demands a covenantal "cutting off" if no other options exist! The reason love is so lopsided in Christian circles is because the church emphasizes Priestly evangelistic love over Kingly judicial love. The message of the church is, "Jesus loved you enough to die for you." My question is, does He love us enough to intervene with those intent on destroying us? The same Jesus who called Peter to ministry saved him from Herod's sword. This enigma presents us with a serious life or death question. Will love judge in order to save? God's love is far more complex than most of us have been led to believe by the sermons we have heard. If God's love is also judicial, then what activates intervention? Can we expect God's love to intervene to save regions and nations from that which currently oppresses them? How can we activate God's Kingly love for our families? Can we activate Kingly love for our nation?

Growing into the fullest measure of God's love is our purpose and we have a path presented in Scripture that leads us ever closer to the Father's heart where layers of Love get established in our lives. When every Layer of God's love is identified, embraced and activated by the Holy Spirit, Scripture says we walk in the fullness of Christ! Walking in the fullness of Christ is our only guarantee of fully finishing the race that we are assigned!

Whenever God wanted to initiate a transition in Scripture, He often released a vision to a leader that led to a revolutionary change in understanding followed by the Spirit's blessing on the revelation. In Acts 10, Peter's vision of *"Rise, Peter, kill and eat,..."* began ministry to the Gentiles.

God's Layered Love started with a vision where the Lord made it clear that the church had been robbed of its nature. This robbery resulted in a theft that must be restored! I believe the church will rise to fulfill its destiny when equipped and established in all five layers of God's love!

◆ God's Layered Love ◆

♦ Al Houghton ♦

Chapter 1

God's Layered Love An Overview

Acts 10:9-16 records a vision that God used to expose and alter religious tradition and ultimately expand the Kingdom. The generation of church leaders that Jesus ministered to lost the power of God's Word through the paralysis of tradition. The God they worshiped walked among them and they did not recognize Him. Tradition slowly anesthetized people until it spiritually nullified heaven's offer of salvation to the first Jewish generation to receive the Messiah. Jesus said in Luke 19:42-44 as He wept over Jerusalem *"...If you had known, even you, especially in this your day, the things that make for your peace! But now they are hidden from your eyes. For days will come upon you when your enemies will build an embankment around you, surround you and close you in on every side, and level you, and your children within you, to the ground; and they will not leave in you one stone upon another, because you did not know the time of your visitation."* The love of God judged a Christ-rejecting nation! How many nations are walking a parallel path? By emphasizing only one application of God's love, have we limited the church and made believers vulnerable to their enemies? The degree to which the Matthew 5:38-44 concept of "turn-the-other-cheek" and "pray-for-your-enemy" have become the sole definition of God's love is the degree to which the church has been neutered in judging proponents of evil! For many years, the church has turned the other cheek to evil and the fruit is the Law of God is illegal in the public square. Layer One of God's love is unconditional acceptance, demonstrated by Christ's sacrifice for us and forgiveness of our sin. God loves the sinner but hates the sin! It is the only layer where we "turn-the-other-cheek" and choose not to resist evil for the hope of a harvest of souls. If we never grow beyond Layer One, we become nicer than God and spend a lifetime in tradition, thus enabling evil. When the church enables evildoers, the Kingdom retreats. When the church prays God's Judicial love on evildoers, the Kingdom advances! To expand the Kingdom, God confronted tradition with a vision. Acts 10:9-16 states,

> *The next day, as they went on their journey and drew near the city, Peter went up on the housetop to pray, about the sixth hour. Then he became very hungry and wanted to eat; but while they made ready, he fell into a trance and saw heaven opened and an object like a great sheet bound at the four corners, descending to him and let down to the earth. In it were all kinds of four-footed animals of the earth, wild beasts, creeping things, and birds of the air. And a voice came to him, "Rise, Peter; kill and eat." But Peter said, "Not so, Lord! For I have never eaten anything common or unclean." And a voice spoke to him again the second time, "What God has cleansed you must not call common." This was done three times. And the object was taken up into heaven again.*

God was preparing the early church for a harvest. Jesus was God incarnate and when we say yes to Jesus, the indwelling Holy Spirit becomes our Guide to life! Many types and shadows in the Old Testament compulsory legal structure were fulfilled in the death, burial and resurrection of Christ. Liberty in Christ was revealed to Peter because, prior to the vision, he viewed Gentiles as equally unclean as the animals he saw in the vision. God, by vision, revealed a transition that needed to take place in Peter's thinking. Tradition had walls that were unseen. God visited Peter to reveal what He wanted to do! Is it possible that our tradition concerning the love of God has hidden a whole dimension of who God is and what He is willing to do for a harvest? Are we paralyzed by tradition? Christ's love is multi-dimensional. It has layers that are each equally valid and increasingly needed. Does our tradition have us as bound to one-dimensional love as Peter was bound to the dietary laws? Peter made the transition and helped gain an even greater harvest. We can follow in his footsteps!

The concept of multiple layers of God's love can be documented in Scripture, but never entered my mind until God interrupted my thinking with a vision. It all started one morning when I rolled out of bed at 5:00 AM to prepare for an East-Coast ministry trip. As soon as my feet hit the floor, God took me back to my youth growing up on a farm in Missouri. I saw myself as a kid on a farm, fascinated by a veterinarian at work with young calves. Every year we raised about 120 feeder-calves for the premium meat market in Kansas City. About the same time every year, my dad would call the vet and we would round up the calves, run them through the chute one-by-one, dehorn and then castrate the bull calves. The vet would sprinkle powder on their bloody heads after dehorning. The first violent act robbed them of their offensive weapon. The second violent act of castration robbed them of any motivation to fight. These calves were doomed to passivity, and because of my young age, I got a good view of the disinfectant the vet applied after the operation!

As a young boy, I noticed a dramatic change in the calves after the castration. They changed from being feisty and rambunctious, full of energy and aggression, to being completely docile. Their activity level seemed to reduce by two-thirds. They would spend their days eating, eating, eating and getting fat for the slaughter that was in their future. Restaurants pay a premium for choice beef. Castration improves the flavor of the meat. There are so many dramatic changes in castration that even the name of the animals change. A bull, after being castrated, becomes a steer. A boar becomes a barrow. A stallion becomes a gelding. The vision ended with the Lord saying, "My church looks to Me like castrated calves. I am going to show you the scalpel/Scripture that was used to neuter them!" One dimension of God's love has been emphasized to the point that it has had the same effect that castration has on calves. The church is spiritually docile and losing ground. This is the fruit of embracing one layer of God's love over others rather than pursuing them all simultaneously!

Over the years, I have discovered that prophetic experiences are best tempered when submitted to Scripture. If we cannot find what we think we saw or heard in the Word, then shelve the vision or prophecy until we find Scripture to confirm it. After the vision of castrated calves, my first challenge was understanding how the church got to the place where we resemble the passivity of steers.

The Lord said He was going to show me the scalpel that was used for the operation. That emerged in Matthew 5:38-42,

> *You have heard that it was said, "An eye for an eye and a tooth for a tooth." But I tell you not to resist an evil person. But whoever slaps you on your right cheek, turn the other to him also. If anyone wants to sue you and take away your tunic, let him have your cloak also. And whoever compels you to go one mile, go with him two. Give to him who asks you, and from him who wants to borrow from you do not turn away.*

This is the passage that is most presented as defining the love of God in today's church. Matthew 5 has become the gold-standard for defining love. The problem is this definition of love has a limited context that only fits certain circumstances. The introductory evangelistic layer of

God's love requires "turn-the-other-cheek" Christianity. But this layer has designated limits. If we accept a "one-size-fits-all" definition of love where we always "turn-the-other-cheek" and pray for the enemy, then we are like neutered calves worthless in a war against evil that would destroy cultures and generations. What if we find other places in the New Testament where we are told to resist the enemy with all our might? Why would Jesus tell us *not to* resist in one passage and *to* resist in another? Is there a unique context about Matthew 5? Jesus was preparing the Twelve and then the Seventy to be leaders by launching them in evangelism. They could not go to the Gentiles and were forbidden to go to the Samaritans. They were sent only to the lost sheep of the house of Israel. Jesus had to complete the Old Covenant and pay the price to birth a New Covenant. Jesus was not accepted in the religious system that claimed to represent Him. The rejection of the Messiah they claimed to represent filled the Pharisees' cup of iniquity, releasing salvation to the Jew first and then to the Gentiles.

The Greek word translated *"resist"* in Matthew 5:39 is **anth-his-tay-mee**. It is a dual-compound word. **Anth** means 'to come against or take a stand against by confrontation.' **His-tay-mee** means 'to remove from an occupied position or to reach up and pull down from a fortified place.' Together the word **anth-his-tay-mee** means 'to stand against by commanding to be removed from a currently occupied position.' Context *always* determines meaning. The turn-the-other-cheek philosophy permeates the church enabling evil! But tradition has broadened that definition, defining love by this passage, effectively neutering the church. Passivity in the face of evil has been the fruit! The problem with making Matthew 5:38-42 the single standard for God's love is that it makes Jesus a violator of His own Word.

John's gospel records one of the very first acts that Jesus initiated. This act was the cleansing of the temple, which was a clear violation of the love standard we currently teach from Matthew chapter five. How could we ascribe to and embrace a standard of love that Jesus Himself repeatedly violated? Are we teaching error or do we have the wrong application? Jesus went to the temple, wove cords into a whip and turned over the tables of the money-changers. The church has emphasized Jesus as passive in love – but that is clearly not true. God's love has active, confrontational applications! We have taught it erroneously and castrated the church by emphasizing this passage as the only standard for love! "Turn-the-other-cheek" has never been God's love response all of the time. Passive love is much more limited in the last days as evil proliferates. The more we move into the last days, the greater the need for every believer to be established and confident in demonstrating the fullness of God's love. 1 Corinthians 13 says "Love never fails" but "turn-the-other-cheek" has failed to stem the tide of evil for 50 years! Jesus turned the other cheek to establish the plan of salvation. Stephen turned the other cheek to establish the early church and in Revelation Jesus rebukes the church at Thyatira for turning the other cheek to evil! Jesus' diverse actions, from "turn-the-other-cheek" to "whip-them-into-submission," guarantee diverse dimensions of God's love appropriate to the evil we face. Tradition has made praying for the enemy and 'turning-the-other-cheek' the gold standard of love, but that is just one single layer – appropriate only in some situations and circumstances.

Jesus' love for righteousness moves Him into the assertive Judicial mode in Revelation. John, the Revelator, saw the Judicial Christ. John's gospel dispels the idea of an entirely passive Jesus. Revelation declares that our cultural interpretation of Matthew 5:39a is a limited "one-size-fits-all" definition of God's love and is an interpretation that even Jesus would reject – His actions prove that! "Turn-the-other-cheek" is not the entire standard of God's love because God *never* ultimately enables evil. Wherever "turn-the-other-cheek" is accepted as the only standard, the church has become an enabler and supporter of evil – little more than a castrated calf. This "one-size-fits-all" definition of God's love has opened the door to the acceptance of sin in the church and consequently the nation! When Jesus was challenged about the origin of His ministry, He said in Mathew 12:28-30, *"But if I cast out demons by the Spirit of God, surely the Kingdom of God has come upon you. Or how can one enter a strong man's house and plunder his goods unless he first binds the strong man? He who is not with Me is against Me, and he who does not gather with Me scatters abroad."* A "one-size-fits-all" definition of God's love leaves us often responding to events in a way that **hinders** rather than **helps** the Kingdom! By growing in all five layers of God's love, and asking the Holy Spirit for His divine response, we assure our heart in faith by knowing we are in the center of His will and furthering His purposes. The five layers of God's love ensure by the leadership of the Spirit that we always have an anointed response to whatever we face.

Chapter 2

Layer One
Evangelistic Love

In Acts 8:5-17 Phillip is an outstanding example of an evangelist. He was preaching Christ. He was praying for people. They were being healed and signs and wonders were happening in the name of Jesus. A whole region was impacted because of his evangelistic work. The love of an evangelist often manifests as the ability to overlook people's sin and love them into the Kingdom. There is also great diversity in each of the five-fold ministries. Mordecai Ham, the Baptist evangelist who won Billy Graham to the Lord, often told the worst of sinners, "I'm going to ask God to save you or kill you – your choice!" Ham's prayers brought unrighteous leaders to the grave! That was probably the strongest dose of love ever heard from a minister but it often brought salvation because it was far from an idle threat!

In the Sermon on the Mount, Jesus was preparing the Twelve and the Seventy to be sent out as evangelists. In Matthew 5:1,2 we are told, *"And seeing the multitudes, He went up on a mountain, and when He was seated His disciples came to Him. Then He opened His mouth and taught them, saying:..."* The Sermon on the Mount was preparation for evangelism. And because it was preparation for evangelism, Jesus taught them, "Do not resist an evil person." Moving God's Judicial Hand could have driven people away. They were going out as evangelists to sow seeds that could result in salvation. They were not sent to the

Samaritans. They were not sent to the Gentiles. They were sent to the lost sheep of the House of Israel.

In Matthew 10, Jesus sent the disciples out. In Matthew 10:5 He made it clear to whom they could and could not minister. In this verse, the two 'do nots' preceded the 'do'. Matthew 10:5 says, *"These twelve Jesus sent out and commanded them, saying: "**Do not** go into the way of the Gentiles, and **do not** enter a city of the Samaritans. **But go rather** to the lost sheep of the house of Israel."* In verse 6, Jesus said "You are going to the lost sheep of the House of Israel and you are going to preach the Kingdom." Because He sent them out as evangelists, He told them to "turn-the-other-cheek" and pray for their enemies. In John 2 when Jesus went into the temple, He went by the Spirit and was led to confront money-changers. And when we go today, we often go thinking only "turn-the-other-cheek" but the Spirit must lead. When today's church approaches life encounters with the only option being "turn-the-other-cheek" we forfeit by tradition, a broad range of victories. Walking in the Spirit means we have five ways to love! Love hardly ever overlooks evil! Jesus did not overlook evil and neither should we!

Ephesians 1 records the message of the evangelist. It is a message of acceptance. Verses 3-6 state,

> *Blessed be the God and Father of our Lord Jesus Christ, who has blessed us with every spiritual blessing in the heavenly places in Christ, just as He chose us in Him before the foundation of the world, that we should be holy and without blame before Him in love, having predestined us to adoption as sons by Jesus Christ to Himself, according to the good pleasure of His will, to the praise of the glory of His grace, by which He made us **accepted** in the Beloved.*

The good news we have for every unbeliever is that they are accepted in Christ. Jesus took our sin. All we have to do is say yes to

Jesus and our sin is covered. He gives us a new heart that desires to live in Christlikeness. But then, we **must** live accordingly. Accepting Jesus while keeping the old lifestyle is a one-way ticket to trouble. I know plenty of believers who keep aspects of their old lifestyle. Even if it is small in our eyes, like pride or love of money, when we approach the judicial gifts, we must be able to stand in the fire we call down. Growing in Christ means not judging others for what we are still doing! The message of acceptance is the message of the evangelist. When we are dealing with unbelievers we are attempting to lead them to Christ, which often requires a "turn-the-other-cheek" approach. Jesus made it clear that when we are in the evangelistic mode, we bless the enemy and pray for him. When we are *not* in the evangelistic mode, we may be led to apply a very different layer of God's love. Once we get delivered from our traditional understanding of God's love, we will be ready to grow in the other layers thereby embracing the fullness of Christ!

Perhaps the parable of the wheat and the tares, more than any other picture that Jesus gave, unfolds the heart of the Father concerning the heart of the evangelist. In Matthew 13:24-30 we are told,

> *Another parable He put forth to them, saying: "The kingdom of heaven is like a man who sowed good seed in his field; but while men slept, his enemy came and sowed tares among the wheat and went his way. But when the grain had sprouted and produced a crop, then the tares also appeared. So the servants of the owner came and said to him, 'Sir, did you not sow good seed in your field? How then does it have tares?' He said to them, 'An enemy has done this.' The servants said to him, 'Do you want us then to go and gather them up?' But he said, 'No, lest while you gather up the tares you also uproot the wheat*

with them. Let both grow together until the harvest, and at the time of harvest I will say to the reapers, "First gather together the tares and bind them in bundles to burn them, but gather the wheat into my barn."'"

Tares look exactly like wheat in the early stages of growth. When maturity comes, tares turn black – presenting a stark contrast to golden wheat. The tares of this parable appear to have been sons of the religious system. In Matthew 28:13-15, Jesus delivers a devastating declaration of judgment,

"But woe to you, scribes and Pharisees, hypocrites! For you shut up the kingdom of heaven against men; for you neither go in yourselves, nor do you allow those who are entering to go in. Woe to you, scribes and Pharisees, hypocrites! For you devour widows' houses, and for a pretense make long prayers. Therefore you will receive greater condemnation. Woe to you, scribes and Pharisees, hypocrites! For you travel land and sea to win one proselyte, and when he is won, you make him twice as much a son of hell as yourselves."

I believe Jesus would teach the same parable today with possibly a broader application. Applying the love of God requires a confrontation with tares in the not-too-distant future! Compromising ministers have much to answer for. God's love for the harvest dictates that just as angels removed Herod, the tares will be confronted! The question is, how much longer will Jesus "turn-the-other-cheek" to the tares? Those in greatest danger of Ananias-and-Sapphira events may well be mixed-seed messengers who, for the sake of success, power or money, continue to compromise the Gospel. As long as the church believes love is always turning the other cheek, the tares will operate in boldness.

The love of the evangelist dictates that we turn the other cheek to people that we believe are close to salvation. One of the phrases used to describe people in this place is being in a "pre-Christian condition." The soil of their heart is open, they have a hearing ear and they are not oppositional to the Gospel. The parable of the wheat and the tares makes one thing very clear. The reason for turning the other cheek is to protect what is being planted so that growth in an individual can solidify resulting in a decision for Christ. The danger of this position comes when we fail to confront evil, and allow it to gain ground in our society. Look at the ground secularism has gained in various nations in the last fifty years. Watch any TV show or news program, and Christians are normally treated as an inside joke by clearly secularist personalities. Christians that believe their only option is to turn the other cheek, have passively enabled evil by spiritual surrender!

Evangelistic love is an absolutely essential part of the Kingdom, and it is mandated by God. But if we are to put an end to enabling evil and move in the anointing of the Lord to reap an end-time harvest, we *must* change our worldview and our view of Scripture. God's love includes so much more than simply turning the other cheek. Remember that Satan, master of deceit and lies, used God's Word in his temptation of Christ. In Matthew 4:6, the enemy "*...said to Him, 'If You are the Son of God, throw Yourself down. For it is written: "He shall give His angels charge over you," and, "In their hands they shall bear you up, Lest you dash your foot against a stone."'*" Here, we see Satan not merely using the Word, but twisting it out of context to fit his own ends. It is certainly a tool in his arsenal, and he is not beyond using it to manipulate the Church, even today.

Consider something as simple as self-defense. It is the right to defend oneself from attack, ranging from simple assault to rape, pillage or plunder. Many have mistranslated the sixth commandment, including the originators of the King James Version to read "Thou shalt not kill." The Hebrew word for *"kill"* is **ret-zach,** and refers to murder or illegal killing. **Ret-zach** *does not* apply to killing for justice or killing during war. Yet entire Christian denominations have arisen with pacifism as their main fruit. Many of the first churches to spring up in America during the 17th and 18th centuries were followers of this doctrine and we still see this passivity rule many congregations.

Is it any wonder that Satan has whispered Matthew 5:38-42 in the ears of the gullible, twisting it for the purpose of castrating the church? When God's people are unable or unwilling to use His Word, the enemy wins in the temporal, and countless souls are lost. Passivity in the face of evil has enabled tares to invade the church with heresy. Preachers of Ultimate Grace claim there is no more judgment. Emerging church leaders claim a loving God would not send a person to hell. The Loving God established biblical justice! The righteous are ultimately separated from the wicked. When the fire fell on Sodom and Gomorrah, Lot and his family were not there! Hell is real and so is judgment! God's love that separates the righteous from the wicked is very real.

One major lesson applicable in this season comes from the Philadelphia church. Revelation 3:10 says, *"Because you have kept My command to persevere, I also will keep you from the hour of trial which shall come upon the whole world, to test those who dwell on the earth."* The only church where God promised to keep people from tribulation was Philadelphia. The reason is they kept God's Word. Every church leader that abandons God's Word guarantees the full measure of tribulation for themselves and their church. Adhering to God's Word is essential for survival in the season in which we live. Choose a church that refuses to compromise!

When the early church faced great persecution, they were confronted with obeying God or man. They chose God and prayed Psalm 2, asking for a judicial anointing. The first casualties were Ananias and Sapphira. Jesus loved the early church enough to protect them from the defilement Ananias and Sapphira represented.

The love of God faces evil, unlike the church at Thyatira. Revelation 2:18-20 says,

> *And to the angel of the church in Thyatira write, 'These things says the Son of God, who has eyes like a flame of fire, and His feet like fine brass: "I know your works, love, service, faith, and your patience; and as for your works, the last are more than the first. Nevertheless I have a few things against you, because you allow that woman Jezebel, who calls herself a prophetess, to teach and seduce My servants to commit sexual immorality and eat things sacrificed to idols.*

The church at Thyatira was in trouble because they were passive in the face of evil. Refusing to restrain evil earned a rebuke. God's way of restraining evil is often releasing judgment on those who promote it. The danger for us is this: When God's agents are passive in the face of sin and evil, they allow evil to prevail. Evil has prevailed in the school system so that in some states girls and boys no longer enjoy the sanctity of separate restroom facilities. Our forefathers built a nation on the Ten Commandments. Those Ten Commandments are being removed from public buildings as evil prevails! What is the church to do? God has a Layer of Love tailor-made for the wicked who are unwilling to turn!

We have seen the fruit of "one-size-fits-all" love in the loss of Christian freedoms that previous generations secured with their blood! How Jesus will gather the tares into bundles is anyone's guess but the Bible is clear – they **will** burn. Make no mistake, what Jesus said in His

Word, will in fact be done! The tares will burn in the fire. There is fallout for rebellion! Those who tolerate sin will be reckoned with for refusing to restrain evil. How we restrain evil while staying in the love of God is a question that many generations have faced. The church in Thyatira wrestled with this problem. King David wrestled with bringing God's Judicial Hand. When Herod killed James, the early church prayed. Since Jesus guarantees David's covenant, if we pray as David prayed against enemies for God's Hand to remove the adversaries, we should see parallel results. Jesus taught us to pray, *"Avenge me of my adversary."* He was preparing the disciples to restrain evil, to deal with adversaries and to face a supernatural foe. What Jesus did in the natural in the temple, He released the disciples to do in the Spirit! But that dictates that we must fully develop in each dimension of God's love to achieve fullness. Fullness of love gains fullness of harvest!

Love's first layer extends the message of acceptance. All of our evangelistic efforts can be summed up by John 3:16: *"For God so loved the world that He gave His only begotten Son, that whoever believes in Him should not perish but have everlasting life."* If a person refuses Layer One of God's love, and says no to the message of acceptance, then we have a discernment option. If they are open and do not harden their hearts, then we continue to show grace in Layer Two hoping for change while demonstrating forbearance! If they utterly reject the Word, then we are obligated to warn them according to Matthew 10:14,15 and Luke 10:10,11. It will be more tolerable for Sodom and Gomorrah than for them in the Day of Judgment! Jesus' unfolding love is very clear – it includes judgment for the disobedient and rebellious!

◆ Al Houghton ◆

Chapter 3

Layer Two
Pastoral Love

The next dimension of God's love is Pastoral love. 2 Peter 3:1-9 gives us a poignant picture of the heart of God as it is expressed in Pastoral love. This passage says,

> *Beloved, I now write to you this second epistle (in both of which I stir up your pure minds by way of reminder), that you may be mindful of the words which were spoken before by the holy prophets, and of the commandment of us, the apostles of the Lord and Savior, knowing this first: that scoffers will come in the last days, walking according to their own lusts, and saying, 'Where is the promise of His coming? For since the fathers fell asleep, all things continue as they were from the beginning of creation.' For this they willfully forget: that by the word of God the heavens were of old, and the earth standing out of water and in the water, by which the world that then existed perished, being flooded with water. But the heavens and the earth which are now preserved by the same word, are reserved for fire until the day of judgment and perdition of ungodly men. But, beloved, do not forget this one thing, that with the Lord one day is as a thousand years, and a thousand years as one day. The Lord is not slack concerning His promise, as some count slackness, but*

is longsuffering toward us, not willing that any should perish but that all should come to repentance.

Love allows time for trial, error, growth and redemption. Pastoral forbearance covers us while we mature enough to recognize our need for personal transformation and change. God is of a long spirit. He is long-suffering concerning our failures in the hope of repentance and restoration. Those who steadfastly, consistently resist God reach a point over time where their continued rebellion fills a cup of iniquity. Fullness of iniquity is a biblical judicial trigger! Forbearance will carry us to that point. When the cup is full, a process leading to judgment is initiated. When Pharaoh drowned the Israelite male children in an attempt to kill the deliverer, Moses spent the first forty years learning Pharaoh's ways. The second forty years were filled with learning God's Ways. In the fullness of time, a generation of Egyptian male warriors were drowned in the Red Sea!

Verse 9 makes it very clear that God is long-suffering toward us. And while He is long-suffering He has still ordained a season where He will gather the tares together and destroy them. The beginning of that season can be slowed or expedited based on our response to God's Word! Pastoral love pleads for divine forbearance. The Greek word used here by Peter is **mak-roth-oo-meh-o**, which means to be of a long spirit, or to forbear. Pastoral love demonstrates God's forbearance toward us as God gives us time and space to pound out the crooked places, apply spot remover and deal with the blemishes that are inherent in all the bruising and adversity that our souls endure as we develop. The purpose of forbearance is always repentance. God gave Egypt 80 years. Coming to repentance is the issue of changing our minds and acknowledging our sin.

When we go to Romans 3, we begin to discover the heart of the message of the pastoral Christ and we find some real comfort. Romans 3:21-25 says,

> *But now the righteousness of God apart from the law is revealed, being witnessed by the Law and the Prophets, even the righteousness of God, through faith in Jesus Christ, to all and on all who believe. For there is no difference; for all have sinned and fall short of the glory of God, being justified freely by His grace through the redemption that is in Christ Jesus, whom God set forth as a propitiation by His blood, through faith, to demonstrate His righteousness, because in His forbearance God had passed over the sins that were previously committed,...*

The heart of a pastor brings forth the message of forbearance. The pastor says, "I know we fail, but I have good news. In God's forbearance He passed over the sins that were previously committed. Straighten up now!" The evangelist says, "You are accepted!" The Pastor says, "Look, you cannot continue doing what you were doing because if you do, you will not like the outcome." It is as if the pastor carries God's soap and water, willing to wash all dirt away as needed. Ezekiel 34:1-10 is a very scary Word for anyone who pastors,

> *And the word of the Lord came to me, saying, "Son of man, prophesy against the shepherds of Israel, prophesy and say to them, 'Thus says the Lord God to the shepherds: "Woe to the shepherds of Israel who feed themselves! Should not the shepherds feed the flocks? You eat the fat and clothe yourselves with the wool; you slaughter the fatlings, but you do not feed the flock. The weak you have not strengthened, nor have you healed those who were sick, nor bound up the broken, nor brought back what was driven away, nor sought what was lost; but with force and cruelty you have ruled them. So they were*

scattered because there was no shepherd; and they became food for all the beasts of the field when they were scattered. My sheep wandered through all the mountains, and on every high hill; yes, My flock was scattered over the whole face of the earth, and no one was seeking or searching for them." 'Therefore, you shepherds, hear the word of the Lord: "As I live," says the Lord God, "surely because My flock became a prey, and My flock became food for every beast of the field, because there was no shepherd, nor did My shepherds search for My flock, but the shepherds fed themselves and did not feed My flock" – therefore, O shepherds, hear the word of the Lord! Thus says the Lord God: "Behold, I am against the shepherds, and I will require My flock at their hand; I will cause them to cease feeding the sheep, and the shepherds shall feed themselves no more; for I will deliver My flock from their mouths, that they may no longer be food for them."

Ezekiel 34:1-10 describes pastors who refuse to wash away sin. The true pastor applies the Blood as heaven's cleansing agent! There is no intent to hurt or inflict pain. Applying the Blood removes the wrinkles and straightens those parts of our life that are crooked. Pastors demonstrate love in a way that will save and not destroy. One of the greatest gifts that God has ever given to the church is the heart of the pastor, because pastors have the grace to deal with the crooked places in God's people that need to be straightened out. Paul makes it clear in the book of Romans that pastoral forbearance is responsible for God dealing with people in patience, giving them space to change. The danger zone arises when we refuse to change or refuse to acknowledge our issues, even after the gift of grace has been applied. When we refuse to take ownership for what we are doing, it is offensive to God and just plain sin. The longer we refuse, the more liability we accrue and the more dangerous the situation becomes.

In addition, if a pastor chooses a ministry-model that limits the biblical moral standard for fear of offending people, then the pastor compromises his call and hurts the very people he was sent to help. Pastors using the "seeker-sensitive" ministry-model must be careful not to shepherd people with untempered mortar, allowing them to think they are fine when they are not! Ezekiel chapters 13 and 34 declare the end of such ministry is destruction!

Romans 2:1-5 gives us a warning that we should not despise the forbearance of God. It says,

> *Therefore you are inexcusable, O man, whoever you are who judge, for in whatever you judge another you condemn yourself; for you who judge practice the same things. But we know that the judgment of God is according to truth against those who practice such things. And do you think this, O man, you who judge those practicing such things, and doing the same, that you will escape the judgment of God? Or do you despise the riches of His goodness, forbearance, and longsuffering, not knowing that the goodness of God leads you to repentance? But in accordance with your hardness and your impenitent heart you are treasuring up for yourself wrath in the day of wrath and revelation of the righteous judgment of God,...*

How long has it been since we heard a day of wrath preached?

In the riches of God's repeated goodness, we are called inexcusable if we despise His forbearance and His longsuffering. Verses 6-8 declare, "*...who 'will render to each one according to his deeds': eternal life to those who by patient continuance in doing good seek for glory, honor, and immortality; but to those who are self-seeking and do not obey the truth, but obey unrighteousness – indignation and wrath,...*" Paul left no room for misunderstanding. He made it clear there was an end to pastoral forbearance and when it came without turning, change or repentance, those who continued in self-seeking and those who refused to obey would face the full measure of God's indignation and wrath. That has not changed in all these years. It is still a functioning principle and still in operation today.

The great thing about a true pastor is that they have the job of guiding and directing people away from judicial wrath and into a place of eternal change. Their heart-cry is for God's best for people! Therefore, they are wells of forbearance. The love that they apply is the grace of God and the continual message, "The Blood is still covering your sin. Now turn from it and do not go back!" Forbearance is God's grace in action to avert judgment giving us ample maturation time for Christ's character to be honed. God's forbearance is always meant to lead to repentance. Whether or not it actually does depends upon where the heart is set. No individual and no nation can sin continually and get away with it! Does 40 years of abortion have a judgment? In each layer of God's love we find God's application of a bigger hammer when there is continual, progressive rebellion!

Preaching and practicing forbearance carries a spiritual price. And that price can come out of our reputation. In Matthew 9:9-13 we find that issue addressed. It says,

> As Jesus passed on from there, He saw a man named Matthew sitting at the tax office. And He said to him, "Follow Me." So he arose and followed Him. Now it happened, as Jesus sat at the table in the house, that behold, many tax collectors and sinners came and sat down with Him and His disciples. And when the Pharisees saw it, they said to His disciples, "Why does your Teacher eat with tax collectors and sinners?" When Jesus heard that, He said to them, "Those who are well have no need of a physician, but those who are sick. But go and learn what this

means: 'I desire mercy and not sacrifice.' For I did not come to call the righteous, but sinners, to repentance."

The religious leaders denigrated Jesus for spending time with tax collectors and sinners. His response was, *"Those who are well have no need of a physician, but those who are sick."* Jesus displayed the heart of a shepherd when He said He did not come to call the righteous to repentance, but the sinners. That statement is pastoral to the core. It is a pastor's heart that cries out to God, "Forbear, forbear! Do not judge now!" Intercession for the nation needs to be pastoral. We need to ask God not to give our nation what it deserves, but to give forbearance in order that we may demonstrate the fullness of God's love as we warn the wayward and distress the disobedient and rebellious. As sin deepens, God's love progressively meets those who refuse to change.

God has five depths of dealing, each one weightier than its predecessor. Those who openly oppose God and spit in His face will find their judgment comes. Just as God raised up Pharaoh to demonstrate His power, so may the world's amoral, antichrist elites meet the Judicial Christ! The doers of evil may soon find themselves promoted to a place where their "...*worm cannot die and the fire is never quenched!*" Secular Progressives, meet your maker as God weighs to you what you weigh to nations! Moses saved Israel four times when God wanted to destroy the nation and start over with him. Moses pastored by gaining forbearance for the nation and judgment for the perpetrators! When the church jettisons passivity and rises to that place, I believe we will see the greatest harvest we have ever known. No sane person gives evil-doers keys to their house except the church, when we misapply "turn-the-other-cheek" "do-not-resist-an-evil-person" and "pray-for-our-enemies." If enemies are determined to destroy us and thwart the fruit we are called to reap, praying for them is counter to Heaven's purposes. King David prayed appropriately for his enemies and we must as well! Whatever happened to biblical discernment? The Bible records divergent responses in Jesus' reaction to sin. He showed mercy to a woman caught in adultery while destroying the commerce of the Pharisees in the temple. Discernment accounts for Jesus ripping into the Pharisees and overturning their tables because their sin defiled everyone who worshipped at the temple. The impact of the Pharisee's sin far exceeded the woman caught in adultery. Jesus' reaction in both cases is appropriate to the sin! Discernment determines whether a Kingly or Priestly response is needed.

John 8:1-6 records, the woman caught in adultery,

> *Now early in the morning He came again into the temple, and all the people came to Him; and He sat down and taught them. Then the scribes and Pharisees brought to Him a woman caught in adultery. And when they had set her in the midst, they said to Him, "Teacher, this woman was caught in adultery, in the very act. Now Moses, in the law, commanded us that such should be stoned. But what do You say?" This they said, testing Him, that they might have something of which to accuse Him. But Jesus stooped down and wrote on the ground with His finger, as though He did not hear.*

The Pharisees were looking for a judicial response. Jesus demonstrated forbearance and appealed to their conscience. The penalty for adultery was death by stoning. Jesus stooped down and wrote on the ground with His finger, as though He did not hear. Discernment dictated mercy. The woman was open to redemption but the Pharisees were not. Mercy to the woman ends with her confession of Jesus as Lord. There was no such confession from the mammonite Pharisees.

Verses 7-11 state,

*So when they continued asking Him, He raised Himself up and said to them, "He who is without sin among you, let him throw a stone at her first." And again He stooped down and wrote on the ground. Then those who heard it, being convicted by their conscience, went out one by one, beginning with the oldest even to the last. And Jesus was left alone, and the woman standing in the midst. When Jesus had raised Himself up and saw no one but the woman, He said to her, "Woman, where are those accusers of yours? Has no one condemned you?" She said, "No one, **Lord**." And Jesus said to her, "Neither do I condemn you; go and sin no more."*

Pastoral forbearance has the goal of bringing conviction to the conscience so that repentance is real. We need to realize there is a very strong price that comes with pastoral forbearance. Jesus allowed the light of God's acceptance and forbearance to shine on this guilty woman.

The exhortation at the end is quite strong. It fits with what Jesus taught the Twelve and the Seventy. He did not just tell the woman to *"go,"* but He said, 'Even though I do not condemn you; Go and sin no more.' The *"sin no more"* is a very strong statement and it has a reason for its existence. Jesus was saying that she would not always find grace if she continued in this lifestyle, but it eventually would take its toll and judgment would come. Pastoral forbearance has a very clear price tag that comes out of the lives of the saints. We endure the agony of other's sins and the pain and death that their actions cause. The Pharisees corrupted the altar that defiled the nation and earned a judicial response. Forbearance has a very high price tag! Israel was given forty more years to repent before the destruction of Jerusalem. As Supreme Court justices legislate against God, will they find judgment in their future? The closer we get to the end of the age, the shorter the mercy period. God yields judgment to the two witnesses who experience the evil spoken of in the book of Revelation.

Perhaps one of the best pictures of the price of pastoral forbearance comes in Acts 24, where Paul was in jail and continually held there because of a greedy king. The king's name was Felix.

Acts 24:22-25 says,

> *But when Felix heard these things, having more accurate knowledge of the Way, he adjourned the proceedings and said, "When Lysias the commander comes down, I will make a decision on your case." So he commanded the centurion to keep Paul and to let him have liberty, and told him not to forbid any of his friends to provide for or visit him. And after some days, when Felix came with his wife Drusilla, who was Jewish, he sent for Paul and heard him concerning the faith in Christ. Now as he reasoned about righteousness, self-control, and the judgment to come, Felix was afraid and answered, "Go away for now; when I have a convenient time I will call for you."*

Felix called Paul many times to hear him because he had one thing in mind. Verse 26 says, *"Meanwhile he also hoped that money would be given him by Paul, that he might release him. Therefore he sent for him more often and conversed with him."* Felix called for Paul over and over again with one thing in mind over that two-year period. He wanted money. God would not allow Paul to bribe his way to freedom. Therefore verse 27 says, *"But after two years* (in Greek – ***"full years"***) *Porcius Festus succeeded Felix; and Felix, wanting to do the Jews a favor, left Paul bound."* It was after two full years that Felix was dismissed. Who pays the price for forbearance? God's forbearance in the life of Felix cost Paul two full years waiting for repentance. Felix did not repent and therefore at the end, he was removed. But the price of that two full years came out of Paul's life.

When God extends forbearance, we pay the price while the cup of iniquity is filled by the deeds of the unrighteous so that judgment can come and change the situation. Pastoral forbearance is a wonderful thing, but it also has a very steep price tag when you and I are the ones 'in jail' to the circumstances. When injustice is being done to us the proper response is praying for people to turn and change. If they steadfastly refuse, as Felix did, we suffer the price. Loving God's way carries a high personal price. For Paul it cost two full years in prison, waiting for judgment to fall. But judgment did come. Felix was removed. Paul's case was expeditiously heard and he was sent to Rome to fulfill his destiny. Justice was done and Felix was utterly and forever without excuse. He had two full years to turn, repent and change his mind but he did not. How many years have our representatives, senators, judges, prime ministers and presidents had to change their minds? Pastoral forbearance is a wonderful thing, but it has a very high price tag for the righteous. Making God's Word illegal by passing hate-speech laws fills the cup of iniquity. Hate-speech laws that make preaching the Bible illegal also contribute. The shedding of innocent blood fills the cup but other things contribute as well. Persecution is growing for the church. God judges certain perverse behaviors worthy of death. He is the Ultimate Pastor and may give long space to repent, but some may get no space. God can choose to shorten the lives of all who choose to embrace certain evil behaviors.

For those of us living in the last days, we must consider Daniel 8:23-25,

> *And in the latter time of their kingdom, When the transgressors have reached their fullness, A king shall arise, Having fierce features, Who understands sinister schemes, His power shall be mighty, but not by his own power; He shall destroy fearfully, And shall prosper and thrive; He shall destroy the mighty, and also*

the holy people. Through his cunning He shall cause deceit to prosper under his rule; And he shall exalt himself in his heart, He shall destroy many in their prosperity. HE shall even rise against the Prince of princes; But he shall be broken without human means.

Birthing a new heavens and earth is not for the faint of heart. It appears to exact a devastating price tag on the church. We see politicians embrace and advance agendas that threaten our harvest. We see the national media dominated by those advancing perverse agendas. An immature love does not resist evil and therefore allows the harvest to be stolen. But a mature love prays what the Holy Spirit deems necessary to bring in the harvest! The primary assault from the church needs to be praying His Judicial Hand to move on enemies of the church! From the day that the Holy Spirit was given in Acts chapter 2, a major purpose has been to make our enemies our footstool. When that purpose is manifested, we get a harvest. Elijah prayed the agrarian economy of Israel into the paralysis of drought to remove the prophets of Baal! We are encouraged to follow in his steps! God promises the Gospel of the Kingdom will be preached in every nation. Then the end shall come, meaning we get a harvest – even in the middle of Sodom and Gomorrah-type conditions!

Chapter 4

The Eternal Purpose of Forbearance

Forbearance has an eternal purpose – specific true repentance! 2 Corinthians 7:8-10 says,

> *For even if I made you sorry with my letter, I do not regret it; though I did regret it. For I perceive that the same epistle made you sorry, though only for a while. Now I rejoice, not that you were made sorry, but that your sorrow led to repentance. For you were made sorry in a godly manner, that you might suffer loss from us in nothing. For godly sorrow produces repentance leading to salvation, not to be regretted; but the sorrow of the world produces death.*

There are two kinds of repentance. One is the immature sorrow of the world which is regret for getting caught and creates no lasting change. This sorrow is self-absorbed and devoid of life. But the sorrow that leads to real or true repentance/**met-en-oi-ah** has seven distinct components, all mentioned in verse 11. Verse 11 says, *"For observe this very thing, that you sorrowed in a godly manner: What diligence it produced in you, what clearing of yourselves, what indignation, what fear, what vehement desire, what zeal, what vindication! In all things you proved yourselves to be clear in this matter."*

True biblical repentance has fruit that begins with diligence. The Greek word for diligence here is **spoo-day**. **Spoo-day** means generally diligence, but specifically 'To earnestly pursue a goal with passion.' And the goal in this case is holiness and the development of God's character. The whole reason why mentors are willing to pay the price that goes with forbearance is that they trust true repentance will take place. Passionately pursuing holiness demonstrates a true hunger for a real transformation. It is a sign of the real thing!

The second major fruit of true repentance according to the New King James is, "...*clearing of yourselves*..." The Greek word is **ap-ol-og-ee-ah** and it simply means 'To recover the right path.' True repentance brings us back to the point of departure. Abram had to go back to the point of his departure when he left the Promised Land to go to Egypt because of the famine that was in the land. God wanted to provide. The Lord wanted to be his full measure of blessing in the land, but Abram decided to go south. He could not resume his pilgrimage until he went back to the point or place of his departure. True repentance recovers the right path and brings our true destiny back into view. And to gain that for an individual is worth whatever we have to endure to see it happen. Genesis 12:8 describes Abram's arrival in Bethel, "*And he moved from there to the mountain east of Bethel, and he pitched his tent with Bethel on the west and Ai on the east; there he built an altar to the LORD and called on the name of the LORD.*" Verse 9 describes his departure, "*So Abram journeyed, going on still toward the South.*" When Abram returns in Genesis 13:2-4, he returns to the point of his departure. "*Abram was very rich in livestock, in silver, and in gold. And he went on his journey from the South as far as Bethel, to the place where his tent had been at the beginning, between Bethel and Ai, to the place of the altar which he had made there at first. And there Abram called on the name of the LORD.*" As the father of faith, Abram had to recover the right path. God is after true repentance!

The third fruit of true repentance is translated *"indignation,"* but the Greek word is **ag-an-ak-tay-sis**. **Ag-an-ak-tay-sis** means to be utterly irritated that we were deceived to the point of taking action to recover the full measure of what God has for us. There is a motivation that comes in true repentance to completely recover everything that was lost – specifically our destiny and contribution to God's Kingdom. The best picture of **ag-an-ak-tay-sis** is David's repentance after Nathan's confrontation. We see God struck the child and his life hung in the balance. David had already been given mercy and sought mercy for the child. None was given, but David set himself to seek it. 2 Samuel 12:13-19 records David's response. David realized this was not the end of the story because God redeems failure. Verses 20-25 records David's **ag-an-ak-tay-sis** as he determined to redeem the failure and get back on track. Refusing to retreat into guilt, he shouldered his failure by seeking God to redeem it! God did in Solomon!

The fourth fruit of true repentance is *"fear,"* or the Greek word **fob-os**. In this application it means, 'A dread that anyone can be deceived.' One of the baptisms that comes out of true repentance is true humility. In true humility there is the recognition that deception can happen to anyone, anyplace and anytime. No one is immune to it. When that lack of immunity captures us and we wake up to find out we have been ensnared or captivated by what could ultimately destroy us, **fob-os** arises. The fear of God is very much a missing ingredient in much of Christianity today. True repentance has the fear of God at the very center of what is released when it flows. Let us pray we will have a move of the restoration of the fear of the Lord that will start first in the church and then go to the world.

The fifth fruit of true repentance is translated *"vehement desire"* but it is the Greek word **ep-ee-path-ay-sis**. **Ep-ee-path-ay-sis** means 'The restoration of a true hunger to seek God for His direction and His leadership.' Perhaps the best picture is Moses, when he says to God, "If you are not going to go before us, then I am not going anywhere. God, you have to be among us. You have to lead us." This is the motivation that puts us in the place to demand God's participation in everything to which we set our hand.

The sixth fruit is translated *"zeal"* and the Greek word is **dzay-los. Dzay-los** means 'to ferment until it explodes.' The reason why we put new wine in a new wineskin is because the fermentation would cause the old wineskin to explode. One of the fruits of true repentance is a zeal that is explosive in its manifestations. If there is one thing we need today, it is the zeal of the Lord throughout the church. The Holy Spirit can be explosive. Fermented fruit can burst on the scene in the same spontaneous way that Jesus cleaned house in the Temple. Ask for a Holy Spirit explosion!

The seventh fruit is translated *"vindication"* but the Greek word is **ek-dik-ay-sis. Ek-dik-ay-sis** is to 'repent and obtain an act of retributive justice.' Acts 7:24 describes Moses in an outburst of undoubted zeal or vindication to bring justice, *"And seeing one of them suffer wrong, he defended and avenged him who was oppressed, and struck down the Egyptian."* Moses avenged the Israelite by striking down the Egyptian. It is interesting that the fruit of true repentance would actually put us in a place to fulfill prayer that Jesus taught about in Luke 18. In Luke 18:1-8 Jesus taught a parable about how to pray. At the heart of that parable is fruit number seven of true repentance. Luke 18:1-8 says,

> *Then He spoke a parable to them, that men always ought to pray and not lose heart, saying: "There was in a certain city a judge who did not fear God nor regard man. Now there was a widow in that city; and she came to him, saying, 'Get **justice/ek-dik-eh-o/vengeance** for me from my adversary.' And he would*

*not for a while; but afterward he said within himself, 'Though I do not fear God nor regard man, yet because this widow troubles me I will **avenge**/get **justice/ek-dik-eh-o** her, lest by her continual coming she weary me.'" Then the Lord said, "Hear what the unjust judge said. And shall God not **ek-dik-ay-sis/avenge** His own elect who cry out day and night to Him, though He bears long with them? I tell you that He will **ek-dik-ay-sis/avenge** them speedily. Nevertheless, when the Son of Man comes, will He really find (this kind of) faith on the earth?"*

Ek-dik-eh-o is the Greek root, translated *"avenge"* in verse 3 and verse 5. It means 'To help secure justice by judgment or to vindicate and punish.' When Jesus declared in verse 7 and 8 God's commitment to respond to the request, the Greek word changes from **ek-dik-eh-o** to **ek-dik-ay-sis**, meaning 'An act of retributive justice, the execution of right, covenant vengeance, punishment or revenge.' The interesting part about verse 8 is the Lord uses the definite article in Greek, "...*when the Son of Man comes, will He really find **this kind** of faith on the earth?*'" Will He find the kind of faith that moves the Hand of God and gains covenant justice? Will He find the kind of faith that moves God's Hand to remove tares? True repentance has a fruit – it gives you the faith to move God's Hand for justice. Isn't it time we find the full measure of what God has for us? We are certainly moving into that season. The repentance of the world produces shallow, self-seeking sorrow! True repentance gains judgment on the deceiving perpetrator and restores and redeems failure!

True New Testament repentance ends in our confidence to judge the very felonious act we once committed. Jesus bought and paid for David's covenant of Sure Mercy. David's failure with Bathsheba and murder of her husband, Uriah, was also a betrayal of his best friend and chief counselor Ahithophel. 2 Samuel 11:3 says, *"So David sent and* inquired about the woman. And someone said, 'Is this not Bathsheba, the daughter of Eliam, the wife of Uriah the Hittite?'" Eliam was Bathsheba's Father. 2 Samuel 23:34 says, "*Eliphelet the son of Ahasbai, the son of the Maachathite, Eliam the son of Ahithophel the Gilonite,...*" Ahithophel was Eliam's father, which makes Bathsheba his granddaughter.

David used his kingly position to appropriate his best friend's granddaughter for his own pleasure. That is covenantal relational betrayal. When Absalom rebelled, he sought Ahithophel. 2 Samuel 16:23 says, "*Now the advice of Ahithophel, which he gave in those days, was as if one had inquired at the oracle of God. So was all the advice of Ahithophel both with David and with Absalom.*" 2 Samuel 17:1-3 reveals Ahithophel's heart for vengeance, "*Moreover Ahithophel said to Absalom, 'Now let me choose twelve thousand men, and I will arise and pursue David tonight. I will come upon him while he is weary and weak, and make him afraid. And all the people who are with him will flee, and I will strike only the king. Then I will bring back all the people to you. When all return except the man whom you seek, all the people will be at peace.'*"

David repented for his sin with Bathsheba and found himself in the unenviable place of having to pray covenant judgment on an act of betrayal that he himself had previously committed. Psalm 55:12-15 records David's judicial prayer in faith, proving the fruit of true repentance qualifies us to judge a felony we once committed,

> *For it is not an enemy who reproaches me; Then I could bear it. Nor is it one who hates me who has exalted himself against me; Then I could hide from him. But it was you, a man my equal, My companion and my acquaintance. We took sweet counsel together, And walked to the house of God in the throng. Let*

death seize them; Let them go down alive into hell, For wickedness is in their dwellings and among them.

David's prayer was answered as recorded in 2 Samuel 17:23, *"Now when Ahithophel saw that his advice was not followed, he saddled a donkey, and arose and went home to his house, to his city. Then he put his household in order, and hanged himself, and died; and he was buried in his father's tomb."* For every woman who ever had an abortion, true repentance qualifies her to <u>pray judgment on justices who continue to make abortion legal in the land!</u> The power of God's redemptive covenant is so great that it brings perpetrators to a place where we, with compassion, can call the unrepentant caught in the same deception to a reckoning. A refusal to repent can cause a shift that activates justice as we are lead to pray it. His love is necessary for His Kingdom purposes – even when it means praying the end of a career or praying the end of a life.

If we find we cannot pray judicially, then the steps of true repentance need to be revisited until the Redeemer releases within us the confidence to pray this way.

The Old Testament word that generally describes what Jesus was trying to teach us to pray is called *"recompense."* In Deuteronomy 32:34,35 we are told, *"Is this not laid up in store with Me, Sealed up among My treasures? Vengeance is Mine, and recompense; Their foot shall slip in due time; For the day of their calamity is at hand, And the things to come hasten upon them."* The treasure house of God is filled with covenant vengeance and recompense. The reason that Jesus said to pray for it, the reason He said to ask Him to be the Avenger concerning our enemies, is we avoid the penalty of revenge when God judges! Covenant vengeance, covenant deliverance and covenant justice are promised and guaranteed by the Blood of the Lamb. That is why, when we ask for it, we, in effect, move God's Hand to bring it to pass. Justice is not complete without covenant recompense. That is the concept of justice. Jesus is teaching us that we are supposed to pray to move God's Hand for covenant justice. We do not take vengeance ourselves, but in our prayers, we put a demand on God to bring it. "Vengeance is Mine/I will repay,..." says the Lord, so it is just a prayer away. Our job is to pray it. God's job is to guide those prayers and then perform them.

Proverbs 12:14 says, "*A man will be satisfied with good by the fruit of his mouth, And the recompense of a man's hands will be rendered to him.*" The second half of that verse is both a positive and a negative. It is a positive for the righteous and a negative for the unrighteous. But covenant justice is real, it is promised and God says you and I are supposed to ask for it.

Isaiah 35:1-8 gives us a very strong glimpse into this realm when it says,

> *The wilderness and the wasteland shall be glad for them, And the desert shall rejoice and blossom as the rose; It shall blossom abundantly and rejoice, Even with joy and singing. The glory of Lebanon shall be given to it, The excellence of Carmel and Sharon. They shall see the glory of the Lord, The excellency of our God. Strengthen the weak hands, And make firm the feeble knees. Say to those who are fearful-hearted, "Be strong, do not fear! Behold, your God will come with vengeance, With the recompense of God; He will come and save you." Then the eyes of the blind shall be opened, And the ears of the deaf shall be unstopped. Then the lame shall leap like a deer, And the tongue of the dumb sing. For waters shall burst forth in the wilderness, And streams in the desert. The parched ground shall become a pool, And the thirsty land springs of water; In the habitation of jackals, where each lay, There shall be grass with reeds and*

rushes. A highway shall be there, and a road, And it shall be called the Highway of Holiness. The unclean shall not pass over it, But it shall be for others. Whoever walks the road, although a fool, Shall not go astray.

Jesus is coming with vengeance and with recompense to save us. Isn't it interesting that there is a highway of holiness with God and all who choose to walk there are safe! On this path we find the Lord Who is our covenant vengeance and our recompense. And He is coming with one purpose – and that is to save us. True repentance puts us in a place to call for that. And it is a manifestation of God's covenant love in action. Pastoral forbearance demonstrates grace to save the multitude by praying covenant vengeance and recompense for the perpetrators. Moses secured salvation for Israel on different occasions by asking mercy for the nation and covenant vengeance for the perpetrators. Legislative perpetrators abound! It is time we started interceding for recompense in the Throne-Room.

Chapter 5

Layer Three
Prophetic Love

John the Baptist, as the forerunner of Christ, had the assignment of preparing the way, so people could hear Jesus. Without repentance, they could not hear Christ! If John the Baptist were to preach in most of today's churches there would be stunned silence. John presented a Savior who judged and confronted sin!

In Matthew 3:1-6 we are told,

> *In those days John the Baptist came preaching in the wilderness of Judea, and saying, "Repent, for the kingdom of heaven is at hand!" For this is he who was spoken of by the prophet Isaiah, saying: "The voice of one crying in the wilderness: 'Prepare the way of the LORD; Make His paths straight.'" Now John himself was clothed in camel's hair, with a leather belt around his waist; and his food was locusts and wild honey. Then Jerusalem, all Judea, and all the region around the Jordan went out to him and were baptized by him in the Jordan, confessing their sins.*

John the Baptist came to prepare the way for Christ. He had one primary message, which was, *"Repent for the Kingdom of Heaven is at hand!"* The word translated *"repent"* is **met-an-o-eh-o**, and it simply means, 'Change your mind about what you are doing.' Many people gladly heard John and demonstrated their willingness to change by being baptized. When John gained a certain amount of notoriety, another group began to come out to listen to him. This group included religious leaders.

If people say no to the message of divine acceptance through the blood of Christ and consequently reject the Lord after being informed and warned, there is another significant attempt by God to demonstrate His love for those in and out of the church. People inside the church get pastored with the principle of forbearance. Those outside the church get pastored with a "Rod of Iron." Again, both are obviously clear in the Word and yet tradition has robbed us of understanding the authority that goes with the "Rod of Iron" that needs to be applied when the Lord is rejected. Shaking the dust off their feet was invoking the judicial "Rod of Iron" and marked the releasing of adversity until repentance came!

It is interesting to watch the tone of John's message change when the Scribes and Pharisees started to attend his meetings. In verses 7,8 John said, *"But when he saw many of the Pharisees and Sadducees coming to his baptism, he said to them, 'Brood of vipers! Who warned you to flee from the wrath to come? Therefore bear fruits worthy of repentance,...'"* John warned the Pharisees of the judgment and wrath of God that was coming. He said to them in verse 8 that the only way to escape the burning of the tares was to bear fruit worthy of **met-an-o-e-oh**. John the Baptist was preaching a Jesus that is not preached today. He was preaching a Jesus of judgment. In verses 9,10, John did not spare his words. He made himself clear, *"...and do not think to say to yourselves, 'We have Abraham as our father.' For I say to you that God is able to raise up children to Abraham from these stones. And even now the ax is laid to the root of the trees. Therefore every tree which does not bear good fruit is cut down and thrown into the fire."*

Can we imagine our pastors standing in the pulpit and saying, "God is about to lay the ax to the root. If you are not bearing good fruit, He is going to cut you off and throw you into the fire." How long would a pastor be tolerated, preaching that today? But that is the Jesus that John preached. Have we sanitized Jesus in our preaching? Have we turned the Jesus of the Bible into a God who overlooks sin? Do we hear about the Jesus that John preached, today? How did our mainline denominations get to the point where they have accepted the doctrine of Balaam[1]? They did not get there hearing the **Judicial Christ** preached. They got there hearing consistent messages emphasizing grace and mercy. And after hearing "God is love" for fifty years with a sanitized definition of love that includes only grace and mercy, it makes sense we have begun to think there is no judgment at all. Some segments of the church really do look like castrated calves. John did not compromise in speaking truth! Compromise might have extended his life, but at what eternal cost?

John proclaimed the Judicial Christ! He went on in verse 12 to say, "*His winnowing fan is in His hand, and He will thoroughly clean out His threshing floor, and gather His wheat into the barn; but He will burn up the chaff with unquenchable fire.*" John was talking to the church leaders, "*...He will thoroughly clean out His threshing floor, and gather His wheat into the barn.*" What about the wheat? What about the chaff or tares? John acted like he was sent to prepare the way for the Lord of the harvest! He was preaching Jesus the Judge. John was saying, "If you do not repent now, the One who is coming will cut you off and throw you into eternal judgment forever – unquenchable fire!" If John was not lying, then Jesus is far different than we have represented! Jesus is a flame of fire. When John the Revelator saw Jesus, he described One who had come from a furnace with fire in His eyes.

---

[1] The "*doctrine of Baalam*" is referenced in Revelation 2:14,16, refers to the Baalam of Numbers 22-24, and describes an ideology/paradigm that compromises for money. While Baalam prophesized under the Holy Spirit heard the words of God and saw God's vision, he compromised for money and helped lead Israel into sin.

When is the last time we heard this expression of Jesus preached on Sunday morning? And yet that is the Jesus that John preached to prepare the people for Christ. How are we preparing people for Christ today? Does the Kingly Christ have a voice in the pulpit where we attend church? All we have to do is review what John the Baptist preached.

Acts 11:27-30 states,

And in these days prophets came from Jerusalem to Antioch. Then one of them, named Agabus, stood up and showed by the Spirit that there was going to be a great famine throughout all the world, which also happened in the days of Claudius Caesar. Then the disciples, each according to his ability, determined to send relief to the brethren dwelling in Judea. This they also did, and sent it to the elders by the hands of Barnabas and Saul.

Prophets warn us of things to come in both the Priestly and Kingly realms. Priestly warnings help us prepare while Kingly warnings often demand repentance! Matthew 21:10 states, *"And when He had come into Jerusalem, all the city was moved, saying, 'Who is this?'"* Jesus was the Ultimate Prophet and cleaning house in the temple was a dramatic display of His prophetic heart.

In 2 Corinthians 11:7-13 Paul writes,

Did I commit sin in humbling myself that you might be exalted, because I preached the gospel of God to you free of charge? I robbed other churches, taking wages from them to minister to you. And when I was present with you, and in need, I was a burden to no one, for what I lacked the brethren who came from Macedonia supplied. And in everything I kept myself from being burdensome to you, and so I will keep myself. As the truth of Christ is in me, no one shall stop me from this boasting in the *regions of Achaia. Why? Because I do not love you? God knows! But what I do, I will also continue to do, that I may **cut off** the opportunity from those who desire an opportunity to be regarded just as we are in the things of which they boast. For such are false apostles, deceitful workers, transforming themselves into apostles of Christ.*

Verse 12 is very interesting language. Paul says, I love in such a way that I may *"...cut off the opportunity from those who desire an opportunity to be regarded just as we are in the things of which they boast."* 'Cut off' is a very definitive covenant phrase that appears throughout Scripture and consistently in the Psalms. The Psalms of David are full of prayers for God to cut off the enemy. In Psalm 37:9 we are told, *"For evildoers shall be **cut off**; But those who wait on the LORD, They shall inherit the earth."* Verse 22 says, *"For those blessed by Him shall inherit the earth, But those cursed by Him shall be **cut off**."* Verse 28 says, *"For the LORD loves justice, And does not forsake His saints; They are preserved forever, But the descendants of the wicked shall be **cut off**."* In verse 34 we are told, *"Wait on the LORD, And keep His way, And He shall exalt you to inherit the land; When the wicked are **cut off** you shall see it."* Verse 38 says, *"But the transgressors shall be destroyed together; The future of the wicked shall be **cut off**."*

In this Psalm David declares five times that God will *"**cut off**"* the enemy. The reason this is so powerful is because of the Hebrew word that is translated *"**cut off**."* It is the word **khaw-rath**. **Khaw-rath** goes back to Genesis 15 where God cuts the covenant with Abraham. Genesis 15:18 says, *"On the same day the LORD made/**khaw-rath** a covenant with Abram, saying:..."* In 2 Samuel 7, when God gives David a covenant of Sure Mercy, He says to him in verse 9 as part of this covenant, *"And I have been with you wherever you have gone, and have cut off/**khaw-rath** all your enemies from before you, and have made you* *a great name, like the name of the great men who are on the earth."* When God is covenantally with us, we have a right to ask Him to cut off the enemy. Consistently, David asked God to cut off his enemies.. David's Psalms are filled with prayers for cutting off the enemy because it is part of God's covenant love.

We are even told in Psalm 149:6-9, *"Let the high praises of God be in their mouth, And a two-edged sword in their hand, To execute vengeance on the nations, And punishments on the peoples; To bind their kings with chains, And their nobles with fetters of iron; To execute on them the written judgment-This honor have all His saints,..."* Executing the written judgment is an honor for the saints. Asking God to covenantally cut off the enemies who are trying to destroy our harvest is encouraged. God's answer to those prayers becomes a warning to the church and a warning to the culture in which we live. Ananias and Sapphira were a warning. Herod was a warning! Should we walk daily so that we can pray "cut off" prayers? How are we walking? Paul said he walked daily so that he could *"cut off"*! Where is that in today's preparation for the ministry? Where is that attitude in the church today? Tradition has made us enablers of evil. The purpose of the ministry gift of the prophet is to impart the prophetic heart of God to every man, woman and child in the congregation. A prophet is doing his job when he demonstrates prayer that cuts off God's enemies beginning with the highest courts in the land. When there is no justice, what will the righteous do – ask God to cut off politicians defiling the land. The Jesus of Revelation knows how to remove those who defile or threaten our harvest!

Two years ago I found myself in a prophetic fulfillment. The Lord called me from local pastoring to traveling, and that began in February and March of 1987 with a trip to Costa Rica to minister to pastors. One prophetic word was given saying I would return after many days and finally see the fruit. 24 years later, to the very week, I was back in Costa Rica ministering to pastors threatened by the actions of Hugo Chavez. According to the leaders, Chavez received two airline flights a week of Muslim terrorists trained in Iran. A liaison with the drug cartels resulted in moving the terrorists along trafficking routes toward the US. One tactic was abducting pastors and ransoming them back to their congregations. A number of pastors had been assassinated because the congregations could not meet the Muslim terrorists' demands.

Since Jesus guaranteed David's covenant of "Sure Mercy" in Acts 13, I taught the pastors how to pray the "Rod of Iron" to break resistance to their harvest. Employing the "Rod of Iron" is our responsibility because Jesus has already guaranteed its effectiveness by His blood. As an example, I prayed for justice. **Axios** is the Greek word translated *"just due."* In Revelation 16:4-6 we are told, *"Then the third angel poured out his bowl on the rivers and springs of water, and they became blood. And I heard the angel of the waters saying: 'You are righteous, O Lord, The One who is and who was and who is to be, Because You have judged these things. For they have shed the blood of saints and prophets, And You have given them blood to drink. For it is their just due.'"* I prayed God would do to Hugo Chavez what he was doing to the church. Revelation 22:12 says, *"And behold, I am coming quickly, and My reward is with Me, to give to every one according to his work."* The pastors agreed to pray judicially and continued using the "Rod of Iron" to strike their adversaries until the resistance dissolved.

Two years later, on the day Hugo Chavez died, I got a phone call asking if I would like to minister in Venezuela. That was not a coincidence, but a divine exclamation point to the judicial intercession. Nations will open when perverse leaders are removed! Galatians 6:7 says, *"Do not be deceived, God is not mocked; for whatever a man sows, that he will also reap."* It is the responsibility of every believer to function as both a King and a Priest. Kings judge and war with the spiritual weapons God provides. Evil leaders are a prayer away from being removed. Learn to pray the **axios** prayers that save nations!

In Colossians 1:28 Paul makes it clear that the people who can receive warning are also teachable. That enables them to reach **tel-i-os**, or fullness and completion, in their preparation. Those who will not receive warning are really not teachable and therefore will never rise to the fullness of their destiny in Christ. Romans 15:14 speaks to that issue when it says, *"Now I myself am confident concerning you, my brethren, that you also are full of goodness, filled with all knowledge, able also to admonish one another."* The Greek word for 'admonish' is **nou-thet-eh-o**, which is usually translated *"warning."* Those who never cultivate friends who speak hard truth will have a very difficult time growing into fullness. Leaders who do not encourage stark truth march toward their own self-destruction and often take others there with them. When a leader surrounds himself with 'yes-men' in elder or staff positions, shipwrecks usually result.

Colossians 3:12-16 is perhaps Paul's pinnacle statement on the subject of growth, development, maturity and the essential ingredient of warning. He says,

> *Therefore, as the elect of God, holy and beloved, put on tender mercies, kindness, humility, meekness, longsuffering; bearing with one another, and forgiving one another, if anyone has a complaint against another; even as Christ forgave you, so you also must do. But above all these things put on love, which is the bond of perfection. And let the peace of God rule in your hearts, to which also you were called in one body; and be thankful. Let the word of Christ dwell in you richly in all wisdom, teaching and **admonishing** one another in psalms and hymns and spiritual*

songs, singing with grace in your hearts to the Lord.

Love is the bond of completion. The Greek word translated *"perfection"* is **tel-i-o-tace**. **Tel-i-o-tace** is 'the bond of maturity' and 'the bond of growth and development into our gifting and calling.' Verse 16 makes it very clear that part of maturity is warning one another in Psalms, hymns and spiritual songs. Warning, in Scripture, has a very distinctive purpose. While we have been looking entirely in the New Testament, it was prophets of the Old Testament that had the job of warning of impending judgment if repentance did not occur!

Jeremiah 36:1-3 reveals the depth and nature of this assignment that comes with the prophetic heart. We are told,

> *Now it came to pass in the fourth year of Jehoiakim the son of Josiah, king of Judah, that this word came to Jeremiah from the LORD, saying: "Take a scroll of a book and write on it all the words that I have spoken to you **against** Israel, **against** Judah, and **against** all the nations, from the day I spoke to you, from the days of Josiah even to this day. It may be that the house of Judah will hear all the **adversities** which **I purpose to bring upon them**, that **everyone may turn** from his evil way, that I may forgive their iniquity and their sin." '*

God told Jeremiah, "Every single prophecy I have given you **against** all the nations - **against** Israel, **against** Judah and **against** every region..." What does that say about prophecy as we demand that it function and operate today? Many say that prophecy can only edify, exhort and comfort. And yet, for the office of the prophet, God said, *"Take a scroll of a book, write on it all the words I have spoken to you **against** Israel from the day I called you until today."* God assigned Jeremiah a big job. Every word that warned of judgment, regardless of date, had to be written down. And those prophetic words promised judgment. They were about adversity. Verse 3 makes that clear when it says, *"It may be* *that the house of Judah will hear all the adversities which I purpose to bring upon them, that everyone may turn from his evil way, that I may forgive their iniquity and their sin."*

Prophets warn about adversity coming because of choices made to embrace sin that violated God's Word. God loves the people so much that He sends prophets and says, "If you will repent, I will forgive your sins." The whole purpose of prophetic warning is to gain repentance and save people from adversity. Look at how the enemy has brought deception into the church where we have leaders teaching, "There is no more judgment." How can anyone read the Words of the resurrected Christ, speaking to the church and declaring one judgment after another after another to the seven churches of Revelation 2 and 3, and say there is no more judgment? To say there is no more judgment, after watching the resurrected Christ deal with the churches in Revelation 2 and 3, is heretical and deceptive. Prophets represent the resurrected Christ. He still warns today. Paul believed the principle of the watchman was still functional and operational and by the time we get to 1 Thessalonians, we are told that we do not even have true friends if they do not warn us. 1 Thessalonians 5:12-14 says, *"And we urge you, brethren, to recognize those who labor among you, and are over you in the Lord and* **admonish** *you, and to esteem them very highly in love for their work's sake. Be at peace among yourselves. Now we exhort you, brethren, warn those who are unruly, comfort the fainthearted, uphold the weak, be patient with all."*

True Biblical leaders admonish, **nou-thet-eh-o**, or warn. When churches abolish warning because self-seeking leaders are afraid to offend, we forfeit our assignment as watchmen in order to gain a larger audience and risk becoming a counterfeit. If we compromise the job as watchmen in order to gain a larger and happier audience, we invite God's Judicial Hand. What we compromise to gain, God's judgment demands we lose.

2 Thessalonians 3:10-15 says,

> *For even when we were with you, we commanded you this: If anyone will not work, neither shall he eat. For we hear that there are some who walk among you in a disorderly manner, not working at all, but are busybodies. Now those who are such we command and exhort through our Lord Jesus Christ that they work in quietness and eat their own bread. But as for you, brethren, do not grow weary in doing good. And if anyone does not obey our word in this epistle, note that person and do not keep company with him, that he may be ashamed. Yet do not count him as an enemy, but **admonish** him as a brother.*

Do we admonish/warn each other as brothers and sisters? We are exhorted to in 2 Thessalonians, and if we do not warn, we are not being a true Biblical friend.

God's love continually warns in order to save. The Holy Spirit warns in an attempt to save from adversity, devastation and destruction. The purpose of the prophetic as it relates to warning is always to save. In Acts 20, we see Paul stepping into that prophetic dimension as he says in verses 28-31,

> *Therefore take heed to yourselves and to all the flock, among which the Holy Spirit has made you overseers, to shepherd the church of God which He purchased with His own blood. For I know this, that after my departure savage wolves will come in among you, not sparing the flock. Also from among yourselves men will rise up, speaking perverse things, to draw away the disciples after themselves. Therefore watch, and remember that for three years I did not cease to **warn** everyone night and day with tears.*

Paul was speaking to the overseers. He was speaking to the pastors. He was speaking to the leaders. He made a statement that is very interesting in light of the anointing of the Holy Spirit that is available for five-fold ministries. He said in verse 29, "... *after my departure savage wolves will come in among you, not sparing the flock.*" The real question for the emerging apostolic ministries is a simple one: The wolves could not manifest as long as Paul was there. A true apostolic anointing first and foremost identifies and causes the wolves to flee. Anyone who states they have an apostolic anointing should see the fruit of wolves fleeing! The fruit of wolves fleeing may be a greater sign than the number of churches planted. Perhaps the sign of the true apostolic may be how many churches you have closed! When God demonstrates that wolves flee from our presence, then we are faithfully fulfilling the apostolic call. If wolves do not flee, then either we have not paid the price to enter the fullness of our anointing or perhaps we have yet to be commissioned into our calling. This passage reveals why the wolves could not manifest as long as Paul was there and had to wait until he was gone.

Verse 32-33 says, "*I have coveted no one's silver or gold or apparel. Yes, you yourselves know that these hands have provided for my necessities, and for those who were with me. I have shown you in every way, by laboring like this, that you must support the weak. And remember the words of the Lord Jesus, that He said, 'It is more blessed to give than to receive.'*" The reason why the wolves could not come until after Paul was gone was because Paul walked and lived so that he did not manipulate people for money. As a result of refusing to manipulate people for money, the judicial yardstick of God was in his ministry and if Paul came into a place where wolves were, the Judicial Hand of God would fall. If it was a false prophet he was lucky to get away with blindness. When Peter confronted Ananias and Sapphira, they went directly to the grave. I rather suspect, based on things Paul said in Galatians and other Epistles, that he continually declared and decreed the Judicial Hand of God on wolves. Based on his statement here, they could not live in his presence. It was either repent or die. I suspect the same anointing that Peter demonstrated with Ananias and Sapphira operated fully in the apostle Paul. He certainly talked like it did when he wrote 2 Corinthians chapters 11 and 12. Paul moved in warning. It is obvious he believed in the law of the watchman as outlined in Ezekiel 3:18, *"When I say to the wicked, 'You shall surely die,' and you give him no warning, nor speak to warn the wicked from his wicked way, to save his life, that same wicked man shall die in his iniquity; but his blood I will require at your hand."* And as a result, he demonstrated the heart of the true prophetic. This is the love of God for the church. The love of God warns and brings judgment on wolves so that they have to flee when the true is present.

Where are the true apostles and prophets today that bring the Judicial Hand of God on the wolves? Dispensing judgment truly is the love of God for the body in order to save lives. Ezekiel 13:19 says, *"And will you profane Me among My people for handfuls of barley and for pieces of bread, killing people who should not die, and keeping people alive who should not live, by your lying to My people who listen to lies?"* As Ezekiel puts it, counterfeits shorten the lives of the righteous who should not die and lengthen the lives of the wicked who should not live. Ezekiel implied going to church and participating in compromised ministries shortens our lives! That also means listening to the true lengthens your life while equipping you to offer prayers which will shorten the lives of the wicked. The true prophets who carry warning are extending the lives of the righteous and shortening the lives of the wicked. The counterfeit are in danger of judgment because they do the opposite. Warning is a dimension of God's love that we need to understand and embrace in the Kingdom. May the true prophetic arise with a trail of fruit following! As we cultivate an ear for warning, we prepare to save lives!

♦ God's Layered Love ♦

• Al Houghton •

Chapter 6

Layer Four
Teaching Love

In Colossians 1:28,29 we are told, *"Him we preach, warning every man and teaching every man in all wisdom, that we may present every man perfect in Christ Jesus. To this end I also labor, striving according to His working which works in me mightily."* Paul makes it clear that it is impossible to present people in fullness, maturity or completion without also teaching every man. Teaching provides building blocks toward maturity. Now the question is how does teaching come? The teacher in God's economy has a heart for the Word. Imparting that heart is priority number one. Teaching can be done by Word and by example. Demonstrating truth by life example eclipses lectures or written materials. Teaching that comes by experience can be imparted. All experience contributes to growth and contains correction. All teaching has an element of training and correction. A son or daughter that has never been corrected is a son or daughter that has never been taught.

How does God teach? Is there a primary way that God develops character through teaching? God teaches both by example and by Word. Hebrews 12:5-8 addresses this issue when it says,

> *And you have forgotten the exhortation which speaks to you as to sons: 'My son, do not despise the chastening of the LORD, Nor*

be discouraged when you are rebuked by Him; For whom the LORD loves He chastens, And scourges every son whom He receives.' If you endure chastening, God deals with you as with sons; for what son is there whom a father does not chasten? But if you are without chastening, of which all have become partakers, then you are illegitimate and not sons.

Chastening is God's form of correction and He is no respecter of persons. The Greek word translated "*chastening*" is **pahee-di-ah** and it includes, 'Reproof, punishment or affliction.' It speaks of the evil which God visits on men for their amendment or growth.'

One of the strongest statements we find in the New Testament is in Hebrews 12:8. We are told that if we do not endure chastening, of which all have become partakers, then we are really not the sons of God. This passage elevates the issue of chastening as one of God's primary avenues of instruction in righteousness. Most of us would prefer a lecture, a sermon, a message or a book. We would much rather hear it or read it than have to endure the chastening of God. The Greek word translated "*chastening*" only appears six times in the entire Greek New Testament. Four of those are in Hebrews, one is in Ephesians 6:4 where we are told to bring up children in the nurture and admonition of the Lord. The final appearance is in 2 Timothy 3:16 where it says that all scripture is profitable for doctrine, for reproof, **correction** and instruction in righteousness. In the context of Hebrews, we are looking at God's intervention in the lives of people in order to correct mistakes, curb passions or instruct in virtue. Chastening or affliction is used primarily to amend behavior. Affliction causes us to change how we think and how we act. God is a God of love, who loves us so much that He will bring affliction in order to change the way we act. That should be fairly clear from verse 6 in Hebrews 12 when it declares God scourges every son whom He receives. Our attitude is very important when affliction comes.

Hebrews 12:7-11 says,

*If you endure **chastening**, God deals with you as with sons; for what son is there whom a father does not chasten? But if you are without chastening, of which all have become partakers, then you are illegitimate and not sons. Furthermore, we have had human fathers who corrected us, and we paid them respect. Shall we not much more readily be in subjection to the Father of spirits and live? For they indeed for a few days **chastened** us as seemed best to them, but He for our profit, that we may be partakers of His holiness. Now no **chastening** seems to be joyful for the present, but painful; nevertheless, afterward it yields the peaceable fruit of righteousness to those who have been trained by it.*

When affliction arises, our attitude must be that God will bring us through it and when we come through we will have the peaceable fruit of righteousness. God wants to train us so that we have a healthy, mature fear of the Lord. We will come out of it with Christ having strengthened the hands which hang down and the feeble knees. And we will come out of it with straight paths for our feet because we have embraced Christ's dealings. Whatever the wounds have been, the promise is they *will* be healed. In this process it is wisdom not to judge others in their affliction as if their affliction is chastening resulting from some deep-seated sin. We must extend grace and mercy, knowing that we all face the God who trains by affliction. Affliction in the natural, while we are here, brings peace and maturity in the eternal perspective, which we gain as we grow in the things of the Lord. We have a covenant and a Mediator for that covenant. The Blood He shed speaks better things than the judgment that Abel's blood cried out for. Jesus'

Blood cries out for our redemption, our training in righteousness, and our ultimate maturity so that we can achieve our destiny.

Verses 25-29 tell us,

> *See that you do not refuse Him who speaks. For if they did not escape who refused Him who spoke on earth, much more shall we not escape if we turn away from Him who speaks from heaven, whose voice then shook the earth; but now He has promised, saying, "Yet once more I shake not only the earth, but also heaven." Now this, "Yet once more," indicates the removal of those things that are being shaken, as of things that are made, that the things which cannot be shaken may remain. Therefore, since we are receiving a kingdom which cannot be shaken, let us have grace, by which we may serve God acceptably with reverence and godly fear. For our God is a consuming fire.*

John the Baptist promised a Savior who would baptize with the Holy Spirit and fire! The baptism of fire seems to be affliction aimed at burning up the hindrances in our life obstructing God's eternal purpose! Saving us from the dictates of the flesh seems to be the purpose of affliction. One of the things that happens in affliction is that everything that can be shaken is shaken, and the consuming fire of God removes both attitude and action that are displeasing to Him as we humble ourselves to His training. While we may hate the process, it produces eternal fruit. God says, "One of the ways you can tell a true son and daughter is not that they are above ever having difficulty, but that they continually walk with the right attitude in difficulty." We know by the responses to adversity and affliction whether a believer truly belongs to the King of Kings and Lord of Lords.

What should we then do with theology implying that if we have faith, we live above adversity? We must recognize reality and balance the error with truth like 1 Peter 4:1,2, *"Therefore, since Christ suffered for us in the flesh, arm yourselves also with the same mind, for he who has suffered in the flesh has ceased from sin, that he no longer should live the rest of his time in the flesh for the lusts of men, but for the will of God."* God-ordained affliction has the purpose of **delivering us from ourselves** while satan's affliction has the purpose of **destruction**. The origin of affliction has to be discerned because it determines the response. Satan-orchestrated affliction warrants faith and resistance as directed and applied by the Holy Spirit. God-ordained affliction requires seeking the Lord for guidance, correction or direction. Faith and the willingness to war and resist is what carries us through adversity into victory. When affliction's origin is demonic, affliction has to be discerned so faith can walk the appropriate path!

Victory is defined by possessing our destiny. Eternal wealth in Christ is far different from temporal wealth. How could we sell a "Health and Wealth" gospel to the persecuted church? Does the 'seeker-sensitive' church-model prepare people for martyrdom? Jesus will weigh the motivation of hearts. Eternal success is judged by obedience! Instead of judging others by success or adversities we should view them through the lens of eternal character. Adversity tests Christ-like character. Our attitude of heart in the midst of affliction is a sign that we really do belong to Jesus. Affliction is not a disqualifier as some tend to think, but it can be a sign that God is working in the life of a person to prepare them for eternity! Affliction is often God's love in action to forewarn and propel into destiny for hearts that desire and embrace maturity.

Discovering affliction as an assignment of the teacher was a bit of a surprise. There are two Greek words, **pahee-dyoo-o** and **did-akh-ay**, that make the teacher ultimately responsible for affliction in the New Testament. There are two passages that point us toward the reasons. James 3:1 is a fascinating verse in the light of who James was in the early church. As the physical half-brother of Jesus, James had a devastating testimony to adversaries because he grew up with Jesus. The Jews hated James and purposed his death! James was a pillar of the Jerusalem church and, based on his prominence in the Jerusalem council of Acts 15, was probably the pastor. He was considered an apostle. Of his various giftings of apostle, pastor and teacher, the office for which He sweated the most for consequences was the teacher. James 3:1 says, *"My brethren, let not many of you become teachers, knowing that we shall receive a stricter judgment."* As a teacher, I can attest that what we teach turns ships and what we pray turns lives!

2 Timothy 2:24-26 connects teaching with turning lives, *"And a servant of the Lord must not quarrel but be gentle to all, **able to teach**, patient, in humility **correcting** those who are in opposition, if God perhaps will grant them repentance, so that they may know the truth, and that they may come to their senses and escape the snare of the devil, having been taken captive by him to do his will."*

Acts 13:6-12 demonstrates how teaching afflicts to turn a life! Verses 11,12 state, *"'And now, indeed, the hand of the Lord is upon you, and you shall be blind, not seeing the sun for a time.' And immediately a dark mist fell on him, and he went around seeking someone to lead him by the hand. Then the proconsul believed, when he saw what had been done, being astonished at the teaching of the Lord."* The affliction of blindness turned the proconsul. He believed when he saw the teaching of the Lord! Affliction is a costly teacher but carries a great eternal reward. The Apostle Paul could testify to that reality!

Eternal success usually has a preparation which includes affliction. Every son is scourged. The New Testament clearly sets affliction in the teacher's realm of impartation. Once we catch it by witnessing or experiencing, we can pray it as needed and directed by the Holy Spirit!

Chapter 7

Forgiveness
The Key to Affliction

In today's church withholding forgiveness is not an option. Most believers have been taught to be afraid not to forgive. But withholding forgiveness is the key to dominion to override evil when the hard of heart refuse to repent. Love, as it pertains to forgiveness, can easily create a casualty of justice. Nearly the entire church equates forgiveness with the first sign of God's love. What we do with forgiveness either forfeits or preserves covenantal dominion! If we forgive prematurely, we often forfeit the dominion that brings justice! Understanding the love of God means that we have to accept Jesus' teachings over our traditional understanding concerning forgiveness. Matthew 18 has been used to dominate and promote unconditional forgiveness within the church. Without the moderating influence of the parallel passage of Luke 17, we forfeit dominion before winning the perpetrators!

We generally draw our conclusions about forgiveness in terms of Matthew 18:21,22, *"Then Peter came to Him and said, 'Lord, how often shall my brother sin against me, and I forgive him? Up to seven times?' Jesus said to him, 'I do not say to you, up to seven times, but up to seventy times seven.'"* The parable concludes with verses 32-35, *"Then his master, after he had called him, said to him, 'You wicked servant! I forgave you all that debt because you begged me. Should you not also have had compassion on your fellow servant, just as I had pity on you? ' And his master was angry, and delivered him to the torturers until he should pay all that was due to him. So My heavenly Father also will do to you if each of you, from his heart, does not forgive his brother his trespasses."*

No one wants to encounter torturers. Therefore, we have taught the church to be spring-loaded 100% to the side of forgiveness. Forgive everything that walks. Forgive it before the sun goes down. We have been taught forgiving is the only wise thing to do: if we are going to err, we should choose to err on the side of forgiveness. That has been the good and practical advice of the ministry. The problem is that it is not what Jesus taught. Here we have an example of how the Word of God can be diminished or made of none effect because of our tradition.

John records Jesus imparting the Holy Spirit to the Twelve. He says in John 20:20-23,

> *When He had said this, He showed them His hands and His side. Then the disciples were glad when they saw the Lord. So Jesus said to them again, "Peace to you! As the Father has sent Me, I also send you." And when He had said this, He breathed on them, and said to them, "Receive the Holy Spirit. If you forgive the sins of any, they are forgiven them; if you retain the sins of any, they are retained."*

He gave direction on two issues: forgiving sin and retaining sin. He said if we forgive the sins of any, they are forgiven and if we retain the sins of any, they are retained. Jesus made it clear that when you and I are walking in the Holy Spirit, there are some people's sins that we are led to retain for judicial reasons. The reason we retain them is because there is no repentance when they are confronted. Many saints just plain refuse to confront sin, but think their biblical commandment is to turn the other cheek, pray for their enemy and forgive everyone. That traditional thinking often enables evil and is far from what Jesus taught or practiced!

When Jesus said, "...*if we retain the sins of any, they are retained...,*" retain is the word **krat-eh-o**. **Krat-eh-o** is the word for dominion. Part of the dominion that Jesus bought and paid for and gave us in the Great Commission is released by whether or not we forgive or retain sin. If we can forgive it biblically, then it is because of verifiable repentance. If there is no repentance then we cannot forgive it. Religious tradition has robbed us of our dominion, boldness and spiritual authority! As long as we teach unconditional forgiveness out of Matthew 18, we will miss the confrontation part which is covered in the parallel passage of Luke 17.

In Luke 17:1-4 we are told,

*Then He said to the disciples, "It is impossible that no offenses should come, but woe to him through whom they do come! It would be better for him if a millstone were hung around his neck, and he were thrown into the sea, than that he should offend one of these little ones. Take heed to yourselves. If your brother sins against you, **rebuke him**; and if he repents, forgive him. And if he sins against you seven times in a day, and seven times in a day returns to you, saying, 'I repent,' you shall forgive him."*

Luke adds the words, "...*if he repents,...*" forgive him. It is obvious why: if he does not repent then we have to retain the sin and take it to the next layer of judicial love which according to Matthew is taking a responsible witness or friend who can help persuade concerning the impact of the offense. The goal is gaining repentance!

The reason Jesus said to retain sin was so that we could take the offender to the next stage of accountability. Love does not just drop people and turn them over to their own devices. Love perseveres to bring them into accountability and consequently redeem their life. If we forgive before there is repentance then we forfeit our authority to move the Judicial Hand of God to eventually gain that repentance. John 17:3,4 corresponds with Matthew 18:15-19, where first if there is an offense we are to tell our brother in a one-on-one personal confrontation. If he hears us – that would mean if he says, "I repent" then we have gained our brother and we forgive him. If he does not hear us we retain the sin and go to step two. Have we been taught to retain the sin? If there is no repentance, we do not forgive it, we retain it and take someone else with us to confront him. Retaining is the ultimate key to repentance. Love attempts to gain the brother. Again we go tell him what he did. If he does not hear two of us then again, we have to retain the sin and then, tell the church. But what is interesting about retention of sin surfaces in layer three. At this layer of confrontation, warning or affliction rises as the option of choice in Matthew 18:18,19. It says, *"Assuredly, I say to you, whatever you bind on earth will be bound in heaven, and whatever you loose on earth will be loosed in heaven. Again I say to you that if two of you agree on earth concerning anything that they ask, it will be done for them by My Father in heaven."* Paul understood this and used it twice in Scripture. To justly function in God's judicial anointing requires clean hands and a pure heart. Personal pain can taint a judicial response. Therefore we forgive personally to qualify to function judicially. Isaiah 11:3-4 requires we forgive in order to judge. *"His delight is in the fear of the Lord, And He shall not judge by the sight of His eyes, Nor decide by the hearing of His ears; But with righteousness He shall judge the poor, And decide with equity for the meek of the earth; He shall strike the earth with the rod of His mouth, And with the breath of His lips He shall slay the wicked."*

This understanding of dominion becomes the foundation for Paul's judging sexual sin among the Corinthians. 1 Corinthians 5 gives us an example. Verse 9 indicates that Paul had previously written to this church and perhaps explained correct procedures for discipline. Here, Paul instructs the church what must be done after the man had been confronted and had steadfastly refused to repent. In 1 Corinthians 5:4,5 Paul tells the church exactly what had to be done, *"In the name of our Lord Jesus Christ, when you are gathered together, along with my spirit, with the power of our Lord Jesus Christ, deliver such a one to Satan for the destruction of the flesh, that his spirit may be saved in the day of the Lord Jesus."* Paul released biblical affliction on the individual that refused to repent. He taught the church how to use affliction to save! He said the purpose was to deliver him from his own refusal to acknowledge his failure. Paul went on to say in verses 6-8, *"Your glorying is not good. Do you not know that a little leaven leavens the whole lump? Therefore purge out the old leaven, that you may be a new lump, since you truly are unleavened. For indeed Christ, our Passover, was sacrificed for us. Therefore let us keep the feast, not with old leaven, nor with the leaven of malice and wickedness, but with the unleavened bread of sincerity and truth."*

An important process of purging out the leaven of sin when forbearance and warning did not work has always been God's next layer of love. Affliction desperately needs to be restored to the church. Paul understood he had the judicial authority to release it. It was given with the power of the Holy Spirit and he went on to give us an example of how that affliction should be released as the love of God in order to gain salvation. Affliction is a very powerful part of the biblical arsenal for dealing with sin when salvation is the ultimate goal. Dominion is released through affliction when a person consistently refuses to hear truth. Paul called for affliction whenever it was needed and it is obvious from his letter in 2 Corinthians that the affliction worked and it worked very, very well. Supreme Court members and politicians desperately need a dose of affliction. Every pure-hearted church leader and every mature believer, under the unction of the Holy Spirit, has the authority to pray affliction on politicians who violate God's Word repeatedly. Affliction can eat the rebellion out of our rebellious justices and politicians! And all this with redemption, not revenge as the goal!

2 Corinthians 2:1-7 says,

But I determined this within myself, that I would not come again to you in sorrow. For if I make you sorrowful, then who is he who makes me glad but the one who is made sorrowful by me? And I wrote this very thing to you, lest, when I came, I should have sorrow over those from whom I ought to have joy, having confidence in you all that my joy is the joy of you all. For out of much affliction and anguish of heart I wrote to you, with many tears, not that you should be grieved, but that you might know the love which I have so abundantly for you. But if anyone has caused grief, he has not grieved me, but all of you to some extent – not to be too severe. This punishment which was inflicted by the majority is sufficient for such a man, so that, on the contrary, you ought rather to forgive and comfort him, lest perhaps such a one be swallowed up with too much sorrow.

Paul is exhorting the Corinthians that their dominion in releasing affliction has worked and now it is time to forgive the repentant individual. He went on to say, in verses 8-11, "*Therefore I urge you to reaffirm your love to him. For to this end I also wrote, that I might put you to the test, whether you are obedient in all things. Now whom you forgive anything, I also forgive. For if indeed I have forgiven anything, I have forgiven that one for your sakes in the presence of Christ, lest Satan should take advantage of us; for we are not ignorant of his devices."* It is obvious that the ultimate forgiveness is given once acknowledgment of sin and repentance has been won. The brother in sexual sin was restored through repentance. Repentance was gained by the power of affliction. Once a brother repents, then forgiveness comes and the brother is gained. When the apostle Paul faced opposition from Alexander the coppersmith in 1 Timothy 1, he did not hesitate, but turned him over to satan. This confrontation released affliction but five years later, in 2 Timothy, Alexander is still threatening Paul. 1 Timothy 1:18-20 says, *"This charge I commit to you, son Timothy, according to the prophecies previously made concerning you, that by them you may wage the good warfare, having faith and a good conscience, which some having rejected, concerning the faith have suffered shipwreck, of whom are Hymenaeus and Alexander, whom I delivered to Satan that they may learn not to blaspheme."*

Paul had several instances where he was pressed into Layer Four of God's love in an attempt to save. In the first instance, the affliction worked. In the second instance, we have no record that it did. In fact, five years later when the very last book that Paul wrote was penned from a Roman jail, 2 Timothy 4 records that Paul had to enter the fifth and final layer of God's love when he prayed judicially against the man who continued to damage his ministry. It is said of Alexander the coppersmith in 2 Timothy 4:15, *"You also must beware of him, for he has greatly resisted our words."* The Greek word translated *"greatly resisted"* is **anth-his-tay-mee**. There is a definite transition in warfare when we find individuals moving over into a dimension where they are actively resisting the assigned purpose of God. It is in that place that we shift from warning to active resistance or the implementation of praying God's Judicial Hand. The hope is that it will be for their own good, so they can turn back to the Lord. Often that is the case, but sometimes it is not. When we find ourselves in such a place we do have a fifth and final Layer of God's love. We have many examples in Scripture of the power of affliction to bring change. The greatest examples, of course, are in the Old Testament. But since Jesus Christ is the same, yesterday, today and forever, we know He has not changed and affliction is valid today!

Solomon rebelled by taking many foreign wives who moved him toward idols. His rebellion was judged by God. Just as Solomon's heart had become divided, God divided the kingdom. Jeroboam was made king and given ten tribes thus founding the Northern Kingdom. Solomon's son Rehoboam kept two tribes of the kingdom. Jeraboam was afraid that everybody would go back to Rehoboam, the son of Solomon, during the feast days if they were allowed to go to the feast in Jerusalem. Jeroboam therefore established a counterfeit altar based on convenience. He initiated feast days in his location so the people would not have to go to Jerusalem. God sent a prophet to Jeroboam to tell him exactly what was going to happen to the altar he built. In 1 Kings 13, the prophet went to Jeroboam to tell him that men's bones would be sacrificed on the perverse altar at which they were officiating. He also announced a judicial sign against the altar in 1 Kings 13:3. Jeroboam was not happy with the announced judgment and we are told in verses 3-6,

> *And he gave a sign the same day, saying, 'This is the sign which the LORD has spoken: Surely the altar shall split apart, and the ashes on it shall be poured out.' So it came to pass when King Jeroboam heard the saying of the man of God,* **who cried out against the altar in Bethel,** *that he stretched out his hand from the altar, saying, "Arrest him!" Then his hand, which he stretched out toward him, withered, so that he could not pull it back to himself. The altar also was split apart, and the ashes*

> *poured out from the altar, according to the sign which the man of God had given by the word of the LORD. Then the king answered and said to the man of God, 'Please entreat the favor of the LORD your God, and pray for me, that my hand may be restored to me.' So the man of God entreated the LORD, and the king's hand was restored to him, and became as before."*

Even though Jeroboam experienced this, the only thing that changed was his attitude toward the people.

Christians should be crying out against abominable laws, every legislator who votes for them and every treasonous judge who supports them! Withering affliction is a great teacher and should be increasingly used by the church to change attitudes. It is interesting how quickly Jeroboam's attitude changed once his hand withered. The king's hand was restored immediately when he repented. Affliction is one of the most powerful tools in Scripture to gain a change of heart and a change of attitude. The only Bible school in the world that can impart the anointing to walk in this realm is the School of the Spirit conducted by those who have paid the price to be trained and are walking in it!

Perhaps the second worst king in all of Israel's history was dramatically changed through Love Layer Four. 2 Chronicles 33:9-13 records the interaction between God and Manasseh and all the evil that he brought on Israel. It says,

> *So Manasseh seduced Judah and the inhabitants of Jerusalem to do more evil than the nations whom the LORD had destroyed before the children of Israel. And the LORD spoke to Manasseh and his people, but they would not listen. Therefore the LORD brought upon them the captains of the army of the king of Assyria, who took Manasseh with hooks, bound him with bronze fetters, and carried him off to Babylon. Now when he was in affliction, he implored the LORD his God, and humbled himself*

greatly before the God of his fathers, and prayed to Him; and He received his entreaty, heard his supplication, and brought him back to Jerusalem into his kingdom. Then Manasseh knew that the LORD was God.

Manasseh reigned longer than any other king. He reigned for 55 years. 55 is the number of double grace. Manasseh is a sign of how off-track men can be, and of the power of God's love even through affliction to return them to the place they belong. The power of affliction brought Manasseh to his senses. He repented and was restored to his kingdom. Manasseh finished his rule a changed man! Many politicians need the hooks of affliction that bring them face-to-face with the grave! When our leaders support policies of death and destruction then they should reap affliction equal to what they support.

Perhaps the best picture that comes out of the Old Testament is the distinctively different priesthoods between Eli and Samuel. Eli's priesthood in 1 Samuel 2 refused to confront sin. Today's seeker-sensitive Christianity often refuses to confront sin for fear of offending people and losing their contributions. Jesus is about to visit church leaders. Eli and sons may not survive the visit. God cannot overlook these grievous national sins. We must confront entitlement, greed, abortion and the entire spectrum of sexual sin! 1 Samuel 3:11-14 says,

> *Then the LORD said to Samuel: "Behold, I will do something in Israel at which both ears of everyone who hears it will tingle. In that day I will perform against Eli all that I have spoken concerning his house, from beginning to end. For I have told him that I will judge his house forever for the iniquity which he knows, because his sons made themselves vile, and* ***he did not restrain them****. And therefore I have sworn to the house of Eli that the iniquity of Eli's house shall not be atoned for by sacrifice or offering forever."*

Eli's sin was that he did not restrain the evil that was being executed by his own sons at the altar. He refused to restrain his sons in two areas: 1 Samuel 2:12-14 tells us the first area was manipulation for money, verse 22 tells us the second area was sexual sin. Verse 25 makes clear God's feeling about both areas, *"If one man sins against another, God will judge him. But if a man sins against the LORD, who will intercede for him?" Nevertheless they did not heed the voice of their father, because the LORD **desired** to kill them."*

Since Jesus Christ is the same yesterday, today and forever, what God did judicially in the Old Covenant, He still does in the New! Most Christians have been plastered with untempered mortar and do not know the Jesus who desired to kill Eli's sons or understand why God was eager to cut them off. The place to start is with the Hebrew word translated *"strongly desired,"* **khaw-fates**. This Hebrew word expresses the intense sexual desire a young man has for the woman he wants to marry. Genesis 34:1-4 says,

> *Now Dinah the daughter of Leah, whom she had borne to Jacob, went out to see the daughters of the land. And when Shechem the son of Hamor the Hivite, prince of the country, saw her, he took her and lay with her, and violated her. His soul was **strongly attracted/khaw-fates** to Dinah the daughter of Jacob, and he loved the young woman and spoke kindly to the young woman. So Shechem spoke to his father Hamor, saying, "Get me this young woman as a wife."*

Just like a young man yearns for his mate so does God desire fellowship with His people. And that fellowship takes place at a pure altar. Jeroboam, in great fear, built a counterfeit altar that led Jerusalem astray in 1 Kings 13. God became jealous over His people and destroyed the altar that usurped their worship. When a man defiles an altar so as to get in between God and His people, judicial wrath follows.

When leaders treat the ministry as their own means to gain wealth, they do so at their own peril. The same God who killed Eli's sons killed Ananias and Sapphira. If God removed Ananias and Sapphira, who were saints, what will He do to leaders who are held to a higher standard? When politicians legislate vile lifestyles and blatant sin into society, mercy for the nation requires removal of the perpetrators. The church has an obligation, when led by the Spirit, to restrain their evil by declaring, decreeing and commanding a parallel appropriate judgment.

In Numbers 14:6-8, Joshua and Caleb declared covenant blessing if God delighted in His people. When we keep our covenant, then God fulfills covenant blessing. But woe to the man who lures people into that which disrupts, subverts or taints that fellowship. Lord, help us see as You see, when Eli's transgression is present. Eli said to his sons, "You make the Lord's people transgress!" At that point God's jealous love demanded removal of the offending parties! If we attend a church that makes **God's people transgress**, we had better change churches!

Is the church being prepared to pray politicians into the full measure of judgment due their actions? Romans 1:32 clearly prescribes what to pray on politicians and judges who arrogantly spit in God's face with their decisions about joining people in marriage! It says, "...*who, knowing the righteous judgment of God, that those who practice such things are deserving of death, not only do the same but also approve of those who practice them.*"

Eli's priesthood was ineffective and did not continue because he had within his ability the power to curb the abuses but he refused to use it. Is the church making the same choice through seeker-sensitivity? Do our largest churches restrain sin? Do they even mention it? Eli's passivity is alive and well! Will God judge the spiritual descendants of Eli? What will their judgment look like? Do we restrain evil? What will

God do to us if we refuse to restrain it as Eli did? Is Jesus as much of a Terminator in the New Testament as He was in the Old? According to Revelation, Jesus is more of a Judge in the last days than He was in the Old Testament! Today, popular preachers become faith-heretics when they claim grace means there is no more judgment. The book of Revelation presents Jesus as Ultimate Judge!

Samuel made a choice that he was going to walk in a very, very different manner. Throughout the ministry of Samuel, we find the afflicting Hand of God in action against Israel's enemy, the Philistines. Samuel maintained the authority to move God's Hand, subduing the enemy because he chose to live a holy and righteous lifestyle. When we choose to live according to God's moral standard, it opens the door to God's dominion and the ability to release His afflicting Hand in order to subdue. 1 Corinthians 11 tells us about our own communion table. When we take communion we are proclaiming God's covenant, and His covenant includes the issue of affliction in order to train for the purpose of righteousness. 1 Corinthians 11:23-27 says,

> *For I received from the Lord that which I also delivered to you: that the Lord Jesus on the same night in which He was betrayed took bread; and when He had given thanks, He broke it and said, "Take, eat; this is My body which is broken for you; do this in remembrance of Me." In the same manner He also took the cup after supper, saying, "This cup is the new covenant in My blood. This do, as often as you drink it, in remembrance of Me." For as often as you eat this bread and drink this cup, you proclaim the Lord's death till He comes. Therefore whoever eats this bread or drinks this cup of the Lord in an unworthy manner will be guilty of the body and blood of the Lord.*

What can we expect if we have communion and we take the body and the blood of the Lord with unrepentant sin in our lives? Verse

28,29 says we eat and drink judgment to ourselves. Then it says, in verses 30,31, *"For this reason many are **weak** and **sick** among you, and **many sleep**. For if we would judge ourselves, we would not be judged."* If we would judge ourselves, then affliction would be minimized and termination averted!

One very important issue to remember is that not every sickness or disease comes because of unrepentant sin. The problem with teaching Love Layer Four is that the affliction that comes in order to develop character and grow us into maturity looks exactly like the affliction that comes for obeying God when the enemy is resisting us. The last thing we ever want to do is misjudge the source or root of affliction in a brother's life and add more pain and agony to what they are already walking through. Affliction is an area that has to be discerned. We have to discern the source. When affliction of any kind comes, our first response should be, "Lord, is there any sin here that I do not see? Holy Spirit, tell me." The job of the Holy Spirit is to convict us of sin. Once we are convinced that personal fault and failure are not the issue, we move over to James 4:7,8: *"Therefore submit to God. Resist the devil and he will flee from you. Draw near to God and He will draw near to you. Cleanse your hands, you sinners; and purify your hearts, you double-minded."* Our job is to resist the enemy and to resist all he is bringing our way.

The very first test we want to schedule is our monthly spiritual physical with Dr. Holy Spirit. Is there hidden sin? Have we allied with an impure altar? Is there any root we do not recognize? The Holy Spirit is faithful to tell us! When we have asked with no response, then we are free to war against the enemy just as David did. One question to ask the Holy Spirit is: 'Is this a justice issue?' Sometimes adversity arises as a result of entrenched injustice. God allows injustice to fill a cup of iniquity so that the perpetrator can be judged. We pay the price of waiting for the cup to fill so that God's Judicial Hand can move in that arena on a much larger scale. One example of waiting in such affliction is the 400 years Israel waited while the Egyptians filled the cup! They were in affliction waiting for the cup of iniquity to be filled. The Lord judged all the gods of Egypt. All the foreign tribes in the Promised Land were to be judged and displaced. The Israelites experienced grave injustice. Sometimes the price for an appointed harvest comes out of our lives in the warfare that we endure. The last thing we ever want to do is misjudge the affliction in somebody's life to be rooted in sin when it is rooted in God's greater desire to deliver. I cannot think of an area that brings us into the Judicial Hand of God faster than misjudging the root of affliction in the life of another believer. It is dangerous to walk with the Judicial Christ but it is also necessary. Paul could not get away from it. He was commanded to do it. We are commanded to do it today. As difficult as it is, we have to do it with grace, wisdom and discretion. We have to do it with salvation and we have to understand that the primary reason for affliction is to save. Therefore our discernment is one thing we have to continually pray about and check ourselves to make sure that we are hearing God's voice and promptings accurately.

When we discern that we are in affliction because of character development then there are two Psalms that are absolutely essential to spend time absorbing. Psalm 89 and Psalm 102 are the prayers of the afflicted. We should study these prayers as a model to pray our way out of affliction and into God's fullness. Every believer should be familiar with Psalms 89 and 102.

Chapter 8

Affliction
The Key to Executing the Anointing to Spoil

Love Layer Four – the covenant authority to release affliction – is the agent of wealth-transfer foretold in Scripture. One of the great prophetic themes of the Bible is best described as the Anointing to Spoil. One time the Lord asked me "How did I pay for the churches I built in the Bible?" I said, "I don't know." He said, "Find out." I discovered that there were definitely two and perhaps a third that could be considered a church-building. These are the Tabernacle of Moses, the Temple of Solomon and possibly the Tabernacle of David. In Genesis 26, the very first offering in Scripture is taken and it is taken for the purpose of building the Tabernacle of Moses and it all came from the spoil of Egypt. When we look at Solomon's temple, the money to build it came from the spoil that David's men took from the nations. So it was obvious in Scripture that whenever God built a church building, He built it from the spoil of the enemies surrounding them. Muslims adopted this principle by building a mosque on the site of victories. An adaption of this prophetically is that a wealth-transfer is consistently promised from Genesis to James. Perhaps the reason is that the love of money is the only spirit said to compete with God for man's worship. We cannot serve both God and mammon. Apparently God has commanded that those who choose the love of money must forfeit their wealth to those who worship God. God has determined satan's servants must finance the end-time harvest. This requires judicial prayer like what was pioneered by Elijah as instructed in James. Just as the Judicial Seat of Christ was established "at the feet" of the apostles in Acts 4 and 5, we can pursue establishing it in the board rooms of businesses dedicated and committed to funding an end-time harvest! There is a seven-fold test for prophetic doctrine which, when applied, confirms beyond doubt God's purpose in this wealth-transfer! God has a plan to defund evil and harvest nations in the process. Part of walking with the Judicial Christ has recently included watching Him manifest in corporate boardrooms where bankruptcy was averted, adverse lawsuits overturned and both vision and profitability restored. When the Christian business men and women are ready to embrace biblical integrity, the Judgment Seat of Christ can be established in their boardroom. The Anointing to Spoil will be the result!

The seven-fold test is something that, when applied to a prophetic teaching, tests its mettle because it requires the word be consistent throughout Scripture – from start to finish. The first question to ask is, can we find the prophetic concept in Genesis, in seed form? Then, can we find it in the Pentateuch? Next, is it in the Psalms or Proverbs? Fourth, did the prophets declare it? Fifth, did Jesus teach it? Sixth, can we see some semblance of it in the book of Acts? Finally, can we find it in the Epistles? If the same thread appears in those seven places, then faith grips our heart to embrace God's purpose. I have discovered over the years that the effect of unfolding that theme throughout Scripture is exactly like adding water to a bag of instant cement mix. It hardens and becomes a foundation upon which we can stand. Faith comes by walking through this process.

It may be very difficult to understand the concept of the Anointing to Spoil without looking at the origin of the conflict that spawned it. Luke 4:5-8 encapsulates the true issues represented by the Anointing to Spoil. This passage states, *"Then the devil, taking Him up on a high mountain, showed Him all the kingdoms of the world in a moment of time. And the devil said to Him, 'All this authority I will give You, and their glory; for this has been delivered to me, and I give it to whomever I wish. Therefore, if You will worship before me, all will be Yours.' And Jesus answered and said to him, 'Get behind Me, Satan! For it is written, "You shall worship the LORD your God, and Him only you shall serve."'"* In the temptation of Christ, satan is demanding worship. The Greek word for *"worship"* is **pros-koo-neh-o** and it means, 'To bow the knee and lick the hand as a puppy receiving its food from the master.' There is competition in Scripture between God and satan for man's worship.

In Luke 16:13 we find the parable of the unjust servant, *"No servant can serve two masters; for either he will hate the one and love the other, or else he will be loyal to the one and despise the other. You cannot serve God and mammon."* The proof of verse 13 is the response of the Pharisees in verse 14. The very God they claimed to represent was in their midst and they did not recognize Him nor were they willing to hear Him. Verses 14,15 state, *"Now the Pharisees, who were lovers of money, also heard all these things, and they derided Him. And He said to them, 'You are those who justify yourselves before men, but God knows your hearts. For what is highly esteemed among men is an abomination in the sight of God.'"* The chief spirit that competes with God for worship from man is the spirit of mammon, or love of money. We could say that the Holy Spirit longs to lead in the lives of believers while love of money usually leads in the life of unbelievers. Every Christian should seek to make his choices based on the inputs from the Holy Spirit who dwells within. Those who reject God make their choices based on self-serving, the dictates of the flesh, personal desire and motivation often reflecting love of money! When a person yields to the

Holy Spirit, he gives worship to the Father. When unbelievers yield to the spirit of mammon, they give worship to satan himself.

In this conflict competing for worship, God's covenantal determination is to give His people victory over those whose actions are ruled by a love of money. Exodus 2:23-25 describes the Egyptian worship of demons expressed by their love of money and treatment of the Israelites. It says, *"Now it happened in the process of time that the king of Egypt died. Then the children of Israel groaned because of the bondage, and they cried out; and their cry came up to God because of the bondage. So God heard their groaning, and God remembered His covenant with Abraham, with Isaac, and with Jacob. And God looked upon the children of Israel, and God acknowledged them."* The children of Israel cried out to God based on their covenant. God answered by calling Moses and sending a judicial anointing. When the people came out, Exodus 12:36 says, *"And the LORD had given the people favor in the sight of the Egyptians, so that they granted them what they requested. Thus they plundered the Egyptians."* Covenant justice demanded that the Egyptians give up the fruit of their demonic worship. The Israelites spoiled the Egyptians.

In Exodus 25, when Moses was commanded by God to receive a willing offering from the people, it was for the purpose of furnishing the Tabernacle of Moses. So we begin to see a pattern develop: every church is built out of the Anointing to Spoil that comes on the covenant people. The spoils of Egypt built and paid for the Tabernacle of Moses! 1 Chronicles 22:14 described what David laid up to build Solomon's temple and it all came from the Anointing to Spoil on his mighty men and what he took from the peoples he subdued. Verse 14 says, *"Indeed I have taken much trouble to prepare for the house of the LORD one hundred thousand talents of gold and one million talents of silver, and bronze and iron beyond measure, for it is so abundant. I have prepared timber and stone also, and you may add to them."* The weight of one talent of gold is 128,000 ounces. One talent was equal to 8,000 lbs. 8,000 x 16 ounces in a pound – totals 128,000 ounces. 100,000 talents of gold equals 12,800,000,000 ounces. If gold is $1,000.00 per ounce, then $12,800,000,000,000 ($12.8 trillion) is the total amount. And $12.8 trillion in gold is a healthy sum of money to build a temple!

There is a picture of God's heart for the harvest! If God did not spare any expense to build a type-and-shadow temple of physical stones, what would He do for a real spiritual temple made of eternal living stones, all made in His image and likeness and far more valuable? Once we come to terms with that issue, it is time to go back and look at why we have examples and promises that the wealth of the wicked will be transferred to the righteous. What could be the purpose? What is God after? The answer to that should be clear to most believers. The only reason to spoil is to take away from those who worship money and give it to those who do not, consequently defunding evil. That is the goal of the process. Satan uses money to influence like God uses the Holy Spirit to lead. Defunding evil is the goal of the process. When the rich lose their wealth it may shake them to the point of repentance and they may have a chance to repent and join those who worship God. It must be one of the great end-time evangelistic outreaches, because every single thing God does judicially, **He does it with the intent to save**. He does it from a foundation of love and **affliction is love** when it removes the barrier to salvation. God has an answer for all those whose resources are their chief barrier! Transfer their wealth!

In the seven-fold test for prophetic doctrine, we need to find the Anointing to Spoil in Genesis in seed-form. It first appears in Genesis 14 where Abram arms all of his trained servants. They go out, confront evil and defeat their enemies in the power of God. Their enemies had taken Lot captive, and all the goods and people of Sodom.

Note that it is just a short time until God destroys the whole of Sodom and Gomorrah. So we have to ask why does Abram arm himself and his men, go to war and deliver all the people, only to see them shortly resume their behaviors that result in eternal damnation? This was a definite example of God's mercy on the people of Sodom, to give them a chance to turn before destruction came. Affliction came to save before termination was warranted!

When the King of Sodom came out to greet Abram, Genesis 14:21-23 says, *"Now the king of Sodom said to Abram, 'Give me the persons, and take the goods for yourself.' But Abram said to the king of Sodom, 'I have raised my hand to the LORD, God Most High, the Possessor of heaven and earth, that I will take nothing, from a thread to a sandal strap, and that I will not take anything that is yours, lest you should say, "I have made Abram rich..."'"* Abram spoiled the enemy and brought back all of the goods, demonstrating freedom from mammon and God's salvation to the people. The people disregarded God's grace! Are we witnessing a repeat performance?

The second place we see the Anointing to Spoil in manifestation is in Genesis 26 where there is a famine in the land. Genesis 26:1,2 and 12,13 state, *"There was a famine in the land, besides the first famine that was in the days of Abraham. And Isaac went to Abimelech king of the Philistines, in Gerar. Then the Lord appeared to him and said: "Do not go down to Egypt; live in the land of which I shall tell you... Then Isaac sowed in that land, and reaped in the same year a hundredfold; and the Lord blessed him. The man began to prosper, and continued prospering until he became very prosperous;..."* The biggest battle for Isaac was to stay in a place of famine because God wanted him to prove His covenant. Will God prove His covenant in a place of desolation? He certainly will! Isaac sowed in famine and got a hundred-fold return. God has not changed. He still wants to prove covenant!

The third and final manifestation of the Anointing to Spoil in Genesis is in Genesis 49:27 where Jacob was prophesying to all of his sons. To Benjamin he said, *"Benjamin is a ravenous wolf; In the morning he shall devour the prey, And at night he shall divide the spoil."* Spoil can start with a prophetically proclaimed transfer of anointing that begins to manifest in the life of a person like the anointing of David! God began to put him in the right place at the right time for His very best. Spoil followed!

Once we see it in Genesis in seed-form, we need to see it again somewhere in the Pentateuch, or the first five books. Deuteronomy 20:14,15 tells us, *"But the women, the little ones, the livestock, and all that is in the city, all its spoil, you shall plunder for yourself; and you shall eat the enemies' plunder which the LORD your God gives you. Thus you shall do to all the cities which are very far from you, which are not of the cities of these nations."* In God's economy, when He sent the Israelites in to possess the Promised Land, they were to utterly spoil their enemies and take from them all that they had. Isaiah declared God would anoint businesses for this in the last days! Isaiah 23:18 in the Living Bible says, *"Yet the distant time will come when her businesses will give their profits to the Lord! They will not be hoarded...."*

It is in the Pentateuch. Now, is it in the Psalms or the Proverbs? Either one would be sufficient. Psalm 68:12 says, *"The Lord gave the word; Great was the company of those who proclaimed it: Kings of armies flee, they flee, And she who remains at home divides the spoil."* Proverbs 13:22 makes God's intent in this realm very, very clear and part of the covenant. Verse 22 says, *"A good man leaves an inheritance to his children's children, But the wealth of the sinner is stored up for the righteous."* How clear can it be!

Now we need to see this somewhere in the Prophets. In Isaiah 60:5 we are told, *"Then you shall see and become radiant, And your heart shall swell with joy; Because the abundance of the sea shall be turned to you, The wealth of the Gentiles shall come to you."* In Isaiah 61:6,7 we are told, *"But you shall be named the priests of the LORD, They shall call you the servants of our God. You shall eat the riches of the Gentiles, And in their glory you shall boast. Instead of your shame you shall have double honor, And instead of confusion they shall rejoice in their portion. Therefore in their land they shall possess double; Everlasting joy shall be theirs."* The possessing of the promise and the eating of the riches of the Gentiles makes God's covenant very, very clear. Finally, from Isaiah 53:12, we get somewhat of a surprise. In Isaiah 53, we have an explanation of the crucifixion and all that Jesus purchased in His suffering for the church. That purchase included the Anointing to Spoil. Verse 12 says, *"Therefore I will divide Him a portion with the great, And He shall divide the spoil with the strong, Because He poured out His soul unto death, And He was numbered with the transgressors, And He bore the sin of many, And made intercession for the transgressors."*

The real question is, are we going to qualify by growing strong enough in the Word to receive it and believe God to defund evil in the days ahead? We do that by what we pray. We do that by knowing our covenant. We do that by knowing God's voice and being led by the Spirit. We do that by asking God to avenge us of our enemies – Jesus taught judicial praying against an enemy in the New Testament. The real question for us is, are we going to grow to the place where we really are ready to execute God's end-time plan for harvest? Evil has to be funded and promoted just like righteousness. Defunding evil may well be one of God's greatest end-time assignments! Affliction is essential! Elements of evil develop in ministries and God exposes them. The right kind of prayer can defund evil. We are encouraged to pray wealth out of the hands of those who are supporting evil, and ask God to reposition it into the hands of those who support righteousness. This is a tangible anointing that the Father makes available. Wealth transfer has unfortunately been sullied by manipulative ministries. The Bible still declares God's intent to defund evil in the last days. Specific judicial prayer is the primary avenue of accessing these promises. We must be able to stand in the fire we call down. Like Shadrack, Meshack and Abednego, we have to stand in the fire that judges the unrepentant!

What we are talking about when we say the 'Anointing to Spoil' is a tangible anointing that only the Holy Spirit can give. An attempt to gain it any other way than by embracing God's righteous standard, will probably bring what Peter pronounced on Simon the Sorcerer in Acts 8, which took the judgment on Ananias and Sapphira to the next step. Ananias and Sapphira experienced the first death but Jesus referred to a second death when He said in Matthew 10:28, Do not fear those who kill the body but cannot kill the soul! Peter speaks of the second death in Acts 8:22. *"Repent therefore of this your wickedness and pray God if perhaps the thought of your heart may be forgiven you."* Weymouth in his footnotes says, "Find out by prayer whether the offense being so rank and therefore the possibility of pardon so doubtful, the sin can nevertheless be forgiven."[i] Peter declared Simon's sin in the sins of death category possibly with no repentance. There is an Anointing to Spoil that can be imparted, but it takes clean hands and a pure heart to both initiate and receive it (Psalms 24). The Anointing to Spoil is judgment on those who worship money!

A good preparation for the Anointing to Spoil is to review Scriptures contributing to a Kingdom mindset. In Matthew 28, the Great Commission declares *"...All authority in heaven and earth belongs to Christ..."* who, in turn, makes it available to us! Romans 8:17 declares, *"...and if children, then heirs – heirs of God and joint heirs with Christ, if indeed we suffer with Him, that we may also be glorified together."* Jesus has **all** authority and we are invited to participate with Him!

In John 14:22. Jesus declared that because we believe in Christ, we would not only do the works He did, but greater! Jesus' prayers raised the dead and the declaration of Peter put Ananias and Sapphira in the grave. Judgment is a greater work! Jesus expected us to walk on earth as if we were in heaven. We accept the righteousness that was bought by the blood. We accept being a new creation. We think in terms of being in right-standing with God! We start out as spiritual children of God and have to grow! Maturity takes time! The mature are not easily shaken! Finding God's purpose is a 'God and Sons' operation! Sons do the work of the Father. We grow into maturity and revelation. Jesus is Judge of all the Earth. We grow into facilitating His judicial will!

In Mark 3:24-30, Jesus taught that the Anointing to Spoil is for the church. It says,

> *If a kingdom is divided against itself, that kingdom cannot stand. And if a house is divided against itself, that house cannot stand. And if Satan has risen up against himself, and is divided, he cannot stand, but has an end. No one can enter a strong man's house and plunder his goods, unless he first binds the strong man. And then he will plunder his house. "Assuredly, I say to you, all sins will be forgiven the sons of men, and whatever blasphemies they may utter; but he who blasphemes against the Holy Spirit never has forgiveness, but is subject to eternal condemnation"* – *because they said, "He has an unclean spirit."*

Jesus made it clear that when you and I enter a strongman's house, our job is to spoil his goods. We can only do that when we first bind the strongman. The language that is used in the Greek is stronger than what is used for the rapture of the church. Jesus was serious about the

Anointing to Spoil. He said so, it is in His language. He bought and paid for it. He purchased it with His Blood!

We need to see some manifestation of this in the book of Acts for it to satisfy the sevenfold test and in Acts 4:32-34 we are told,

> *Now the multitude of those who believed were of one heart and one soul; neither did anyone say that any of the things he possessed was his own, but they had all things in common. And with great power the apostles gave witness to the resurrection of the Lord Jesus. And great grace was upon them all. Nor was there anyone among them who lacked; for all who were possessors of lands or houses sold them, and brought the proceeds of the things that were sold,...*

When God's anointing is so strong on a people that nobody says that anything he has is his own, you know that the miraculous is operational. Two people attempted to join the group with a different heart. Their names were Ananias and Sapphira and they did not live long. Was this the same anointing that came on the Hebrews when God told them to take whatever they wanted in the exodus from Egypt? If the fear of God is the common denominator between the Old and New Testament, then it is an agent of spoil. The Anointing to Spoil appears to be New Testament.

Finally, to pass the last test, we need to find it somewhere in the Epistles. In James 5:1-3 we are told, *"Come now, you rich, weep and howl for your miseries that are coming upon you! Your riches are corrupted, and your garments are moth-eaten. Your gold and silver are corroded, and their corrosion will be a witness against you and will eat your flesh like fire. You have heaped up treasure in the last days."* All those who have hoarded wealth are headed for fiery circumstances. God saw wealth accumulation in the last days as an issue deserving judicial recompense. Elijah is our example. He prayed the economy closed and production stopped. Elijah confronted evil by praying the economy of Israel into a standstill. He completely defunded the champions of evil in his generation and then put them to death. Is God serious about the Anointing to Spoil? Is He serious about gaining an end-time harvest? Could this be one of the keys to the Jewish harvest? Psalm 2 says, *"Ask me and I will give you the nations..."* I believe that one of the greatest weapons for securing salvation in the last days is the love of God that afflicts. Affliction manifests in people losing their substance, where they only have one place to turn - to the Lord Jesus! The God of Heaven, who created the earth, is ready to receive a harvest! May the church arise into this level of God's anointing and see the greatest harvest we have ever known! Hoarding, as identified in Scripture, is not a house so full it is unmanageable, but rather a person who accumulates wealth that they dedicate to promoting what God hates. When hoarding is applied to believers, it refers to refusing to obey God in giving so that the wealth cries out against its owner. Those who hoard in disobedience will ultimately wish the rocks had fallen on them! According to Revelation 6:15,16, praying afflicting fire on hoarders could release a transfer of wealth. God promises to transfer that which is selfishly hoarded.

Jesus challenged us to walk in this realm in Luke 18:1-8,

Then He spoke a parable to them, that men always ought to pray and not lose heart, saying: "There was in a certain city a judge who did not fear God nor regard man. Now there was a widow in that city; and she came to him, saying, 'Get justice for me from my adversary.' And he would not for a while; but afterward he said within himself, 'Though I do not fear God nor regard man, yet because this widow troubles me I will avenge her, lest by her continual coming she weary me.'" Then the Lord said, "Hear what the unjust judge said. And shall God not avenge His own elect who cry out day and night to Him, though He bears long with them? I tell you that He will avenge them speedily. Nevertheless, when the Son of Man comes, will He really find faith on the earth?"

How do we know when we qualify for a wealth transfer defunding evil? **Ek-dik-eh-o** is the Greek word describing the widow's prayer. It means, 'vindicate, punish or help secure justice by judgment.' Paul walked in this realm and urged the Corinthians to follow his example and walk there. In 2 Corinthians 10:1-6 Paul teaches us how to qualify,

Now I, Paul, myself am pleading with you by the meekness and gentleness of Christ – who in presence am lowly among you, but being absent am bold toward you. But I beg you that when I am present I may not be bold with that confidence by which I intend to be bold against some, who think of us as if we walked according to the flesh. For though we walk in the flesh, we do not war according to the flesh. For the weapons of our warfare are not carnal but mighty in God for pulling down strongholds, casting down arguments and every high thing that exalts itself against the knowledge of God, bringing every thought into captivity to the obedience of Christ, and being ready to punish all disobedience when your obedience is fulfilled.

The Greek word for *"punish"* in verse 6 is **ek-dik-eh-o**. The very same word used for the widow's prayer! What has God asked of us that we have left undone? When we complete what God asks, we qualify to ask biblical justice, knowing that God's timing is sovereign. The two witnesses of Revelation 11 execute justice as often as they will. Wouldn't it be fulfilling to walk with God in a place where He trusted us with His justice? If the two witnesses represent the **Kingly** and **Priestly** anointing, we may be much closer than we think.

Financial affliction may well be one of the greatest open doors to salvation that exists in the last days. Because money is the counterfeit to the Holy Spirit, in competing for worship, any disruption in the financial flow makes people vulnerable and open to reconsider their ways.

I was ministering in Dallas to businessmen about covenant justice. A contractor shared how he was losing 90% of his bids. He discovered his chief competitor was bidding at cost and overbilling to make up the dollars needed for profit. I prayed covenant justice. Two months later, the pastor called to share that the competitor had been caught overbilling and was fired from a multi-million dollar project. The young man I prayed for was asked to finish the contract. About a year later, the dishonest competitor was complaining about losing all his bids. The young man I had prayed for shared about praying God's justice and that judgment was falling on the dishonest tactics. The dishonest contractor repented and returned to the Lord! Financial affliction opens a path to salvation!

Chapter 9

Layer Five
Apostolic Love

The fifth and final Layer of God's love is represented in the New Testament by the ministry gift of the Apostle. Revelation 2:2,3 says in Jesus' message to Ephesus, *"I know your works, your labor, your patience, and that you cannot bear those who are evil. And you have tested those who say they are apostles and are not, and have found them liars; and you have persevered and have patience, and have labored for My name's sake and have not become weary."* The church at Ephesus understood there was a test that went with apostolic authority.

Perhaps that test originated in the actions of Acts 5:1-11 which says,

> *But a certain man named Ananias, with Sapphira his wife, sold a possession. And he kept back part of the proceeds, his wife also being aware of it, and brought a certain part and laid it at the apostles' feet. But Peter said, "Ananias, why has Satan filled your heart to lie to the Holy Spirit and keep back part of the price of the land for yourself? While it remained, was it not your own? And after it was sold, was it not in your own control? Why have you conceived this thing in your heart? You have not lied to men but to God." Then Ananias, hearing these words, fell down*

and breathed his last. So great fear came upon all those who heard these things. And the young men arose and wrapped him up, carried him out, and buried him. Now it was about three hours later when his wife came in, not knowing what had happened. And Peter answered her, "Tell me whether you sold the land for so much?" She said, "Yes, for so much." Then Peter said to her, "How is it that you have agreed together to test the Spirit of the Lord? Look, the feet of those who have buried your husband are at the door, and they will carry you out." Then immediately she fell down at his feet and breathed her last. And the young men came in and found her dead, and carrying her out, buried her by her husband. So great fear came upon all the church and upon all who heard these things.

There is a reason that verse 13 tells us, *"Yet none of the rest dared join them, but the people esteemed them highly."* One aspect of the apostolic call was terminating the resistance. This anointing is a manifestation of what Peter declared when the Holy Spirit came in Acts 2:34-36. Peter said it this way, *"For David did not ascend into the heavens, but he says himself: 'The LORD said to my Lord, 'Sit at My right hand, Till I make Your enemies Your footstool.'" Therefore let all the house of Israel know assuredly that God has made this Jesus, whom you crucified, both Lord and Christ."*

Psalm 110 describes the fruit expected when the Holy Spirit came in Acts 2 on the day of Pentecost. The Holy Spirit leads us into the Kingly anointing where we project kingdom rule! Jesus bought and paid for two distinctive ministries. He became the **koo-ree-os**, the Owner, Possessor and Disposer or King/Judge of all the Earth. He was also the **khris-tos**, the Anointed Savior-Priest. By sitting at the right Hand of God, Jesus had been made both Judge and Savior. The apostles represented Jesus the Judge in a very unique way. They possessed the anointing to terminate those who refused to release their evil assignment. Those who stood in opposition to God's purpose and plan faced a determined Judge! The apostles found themselves doing what a king had to do in the Old Testament. In 1 Samuel 8:4,5 the people were asking for a king. Verses 4,5 state, *"Then all the elders of Israel gathered together and came to Samuel at Ramah, and said to him, 'Look, you are old, and your sons do not walk in your ways. Now make us a king to judge us like all the nations.'"* Being asked again in verses 19 and 20, *"Nevertheless the people refused to obey the voice of Samuel; and they said, 'No, but we will have a king over us, that we also may be like all the nations, and that our king may judge us and go out before us and fight our battles.'"* Verse 20 is very explicit about the purpose of kings: their job was to rule, to judge and to go to war.

When we look at the resurrected Christ returning in Revelation 19, we are told in verse 11, *"Now I saw heaven opened, and behold, a white horse. And He who sat on him was called Faithful and True, and in righteousness He judges and makes war."* Jesus is coming back on a white horse and the first things that are said about Him comprise the King's anointing. He is judging and He is making war. If there is a deficit in our development, it is that we have spent so much time developing the priestly that very few have the confidence to act judicially as a spiritual king! **God loves His Body and the harvest Jesus died for enough to terminate those who are intent on destroying it!** This is the fruit of the anointing to judge and make war. Where is this anointing active? It has manifested throughout church history and operates today through those in the church who purify their hearts and follow the Spirit. Jesus has it. It is available to the church. Peter walked in it. Paul walked in it. Some of us have been dragged into it.

During the Afghanistan war, the leading clerics (Imams) in a Muslim nation critical to the war effort issued a fatwā (judgment up to and including death that "faithful" Muslims must fulfill) against the main Christian leader and he was killed. The same Imams proceeded to issue another fatwā against the number two Christian leader (the second highest Christian leader in the land). The government of the country told this man to leave because they could not protect him. The Christian leader came to America and visited a church in Southern California, where biblical justice was understood. Several church leaders prayed judicially over this minister. They demanded covenant justice and prayed Layer Five of God's love on his persecutors. Within a few days the government contacted the pastor, saying it was safe for him to return home. Apparently the Imams who issued the fatwā became 'collateral damage' of a nearby US drone strike! Covenant justice restored the pastor to his ministry!

This anointing is alive and well. It is available to every believer. According to Revelation 1:6, He, "...*has made us kings and priests to His God and Father, to Him be glory and dominion forever and ever. Amen.*" The stunning thing about Scripture is that Jesus died to make available the anointing to walk with Him as King and as Priest. The church at Ephesus would not abide anyone who said they had an apostolic ministry who did not have this fruit in their life. Why do apostles exist? Their job is to bring the church into fullness. If we walk in the fullness of Christ then we must represent Jesus, as both Savior and King. If we cannot pray the purveyors of evil into the grave when they refuse to repent, then we are not fully developed in the kingly love of God. The reason God judges, the reason He wars, the reason He terminates is because there are purveyors of evil who refuse to repent and who are determined to destroy our God-given harvest field. Angels remove the tares at harvest time. When government mandates teaching small children what God abhors, we have a monumental spiritual conflict. If politicians support antichrist positions, at the minimum it warrants Kingly Judicial intercession releasing angels who terminate. When the early church prayed not only was Peter sovereignly removed from jail, but an angel with terminating authority visited Herod. This is New Testament justice and must be restored to the church. What Herod attempted to do to Peter was done to Herod in Acts 12:23! This is covenant justice. Those who intend to silence the church with hate-speech law should themselves be prayed into silence! Covenant justice is available!

Apostolic authority was demonstrated by prayer that released angels to terminate. God's love for the children dictates that the church pray covenant justice on the perpetrators of evil. God hates certain sin enough to judge it worthy of death. Revelation 2:15,16 states, *"'Nevertheless I have a few things against you, because you allow that woman Jezebel, who calls herself a prophetess, to teach and seduce My servants to commit sexual immorality and eat things sacrificed to idols. And I gave her time to repent of her sexual immorality, and she did not repent. Indeed I will cast her into a sickbed, and those who commit adultery with her into great tribulation, unless they repent of their deeds. I will kill her children with death, and all the churches shall know that I am He who searches the minds and hearts. And I will give to each one of you according to your works.'"* "According to your works..."covers the entire spectrum of covenant justice! In this passage, Jesus also outlines criteria for termination! Leaders in denominations who ordain homosexual priests could easily face the Eternal Terminator. God hates sin that destroys people eternally. The practice of sexual sin with no repentance guarantees a place in hell forever. Promoting behavior that brings God's judgment brings spiritual jeopardy. Allowing sin free reign risks losing the nation. The Judge of all the earth is looking at nations and their choices! Liberal politicians who promote antichrist policies do so at their own peril. God loves the church enough to terminate our enemies! God's love does not allow evil to destroy a future harvest of souls. Just as a father and mother protect young children from predators, so God protects through termination when the predator consistently refuses to repent. The Holy Spirit may very well lead us to pray termination!

The reason God judges, the reason He wars, the reason He terminates is because there are purveyors of evil who refuse to repent and who are hell bent on multiplying themselves and infecting and destroying as many as possible. Every individual in government who is responsible for voting sin into law deserves to meet Jesus the Terminator. They should be prayed into termination. Every politician who supports legalizing that which the Bible calls sin, whether Democrat or Republican, should be prayed into termination. When cultures adopt what God forbids, they will start to lose cities. People who promote perversion are impeding the harvest field and both the Old and New Testament state that the cleansing penalty can be termination!

Romans 1 is very clear about this issue. In verses 24-32 it says,

*Therefore God also **gave them up** to uncleanness, in the lusts of their hearts, to dishonor their bodies among themselves, who exchanged the truth of God for the lie, and worshiped and served the creature rather than the Creator, who is blessed forever. Amen. For this reason God **gave them up** to vile passions. For even their women exchanged the natural use for what is against nature. Likewise also the men, leaving the natural use of the woman, burned in their lust for one another, men with men committing what is shameful, and receiving in themselves the penalty of their error which was **due**. And even as they did not like to retain God in their knowledge, God gave them over to a debased mind, to do those things which are not fitting; being filled with all unrighteousness, sexual immorality, wickedness, covetousness, maliciousness; full of envy, **murder**, strife, deceit, evil-mindedness; they are whisperers, backbiters,*

haters of God, violent, *proud, boasters, inventors of evil things, disobedient to parents, undiscerning, untrustworthy, unloving, unforgiving, unmerciful; who, knowing the righteous judgment of God, that those who practice such things are* **deserving of death,** *not only do the same but also approve of those who practice them.*

The apostolic anointing, as it emerges in the church, will be visibly seen when the ones God has given over to a debased mind, can no longer find repentance and have to be terminated. When God bares His Judicial Arm, perpetrators repent or die! 1 Peter 4:15 tells us, *"But let none of you suffer as a murderer, a thief, an evildoer, or as a busybody in other people's matters."* It is obvious we are not to lift our hand against these individuals in the natural but we are to pray the termination of God on their heads because they defile the culture and bring judgment on the land. If we approve their evil deeds by silence, then we qualify for God's Judicial Hand along with them! The other option is pray as David prayed in Psalm 7:6-16.

Arise, O Lord, in Your anger; Lift Yourself up because of the rage of my enemies; Rise up for me to the judgment You have commanded! So the congregation of the peoples shall surround You; For their sakes, therefore, return on high. The Lord shall judge the peoples; Judge me, O Lord, according to my righteousness, And according to my integrity within me. Oh, let the wickedness of the wicked come to an end, But establish the just; For the righteous God tests the hearts and minds. My defense is of God, Who saves the upright in heart. God is a just judge, And God is angry with the wicked every day. If he does not turn back, He will sharpen His sword; He bends His bow and makes it ready. He also prepares for Himself instruments of death; He makes His arrows into fiery shafts Behold, the wicked brings forth iniquity; Yes, he conceives trouble and brings forth falsehood. He made a pit and dug it out, And has fallen into the ditch which he made. His trouble shall return upon his own head, And his violent dealing shall come down on his own crown.

If the current avalanche of evil goes unchecked, it will cost us entire cities being judged and removed, just as Sodom and Gomorrah were. No culture can promote what God abhors and not come into utter, dramatic and devastating judgment. The love of God intervenes to gain a measure of salvation. Moses saved Israel four times by praying justice on the perpetrators and mercy for the nation. If the church fails, then we forfeit the harvest promised. Our Bible tells us the church does not fail. Daniel saw the worst season ever to befall humanity and he said, *"...but the people who know their God shall be strong, and carry out great exploits."* (Daniel 11:32b) The love of God, in Scripture, intervenes judicially to save nations by removing the perpetrators. Patterns in Scripture are given to encourage us to trust for parallel results! It would be so simple if perpetrators would repent, but when they harden their hearts in rebellion then they earn a penalty for rejecting the Word. Isaiah 5:20-25 describes the process. Jesus pronounced those woes in Matthew 23 from Isaiah 5. It first happened spiritually. The religious system rejected its own Messiah and lost all authority. Jesus became the foundation stone for a New Covenant. Jerusalem and the temple were destroyed 40 years later. Prayer patterns exist in the Old Testament.

Each time God wanted to destroy Israel, Moses intervened by intercession. God is no respecter of persons and we can also go there with the Lord. In Exodus 32, Moses came down from the mountain and God was ready to destroy the congregation and start over with him. Verse 10 says, *"Now therefore, let Me alone, that My wrath may burn hot against them and I may consume them. And I will make of you a great nation."* What did Moses do? Verses 25-28 tells us,

> *Now when Moses saw that the people were unrestrained (for Aaron had not restrained them, to their shame among their enemies), then Moses stood in the entrance of the camp, and said, "Whoever is on the LORD's side – come to me!" And all the sons of Levi gathered themselves together to him. And he said to them, "Thus says the LORD God of Israel: 'Let every man put his sword on his side, and go in and out from entrance to entrance throughout the camp, and let every man kill his brother, every man his companion, and every man his neighbor.'" So the sons of Levi did according to the word of Moses. And about three thousand men of the people fell that day.*

Will the Judicial Christ walk through nations in the last days?

Everyone committing sexual sin died. Moses asked all those who were on his side to step over the line. The tribe of Levi answered the call. What the tribe of Levi had to do was execute apostolic authority and deal with the perpetrators even in their own family because of immorality. The tribe of Levi was willing to confront and remove the evil, and as a result they were given the priesthood. What it means to walk as a Priest before the Lord is that we are willing to pray perpetrators who refuse to repent into their eternal reward. Declare it, decree it, prophecy it and call it forth as led by the Holy Spirit. It is a part of being a King. From a New Testament perspective, Jesus commanded the Twelve and the Seventy to, by the Spirit, pronounce covenantal justice on those who rejected the Word! The emergence of the apostolic ministry has a foundational purpose of restoring this judicial understanding to the church. We cannot have an end-time harvest if we are not willing to pray the tares into termination because they are destroying the harvest field.

In Numbers 16, Moses' own leadership was under assault by Korah, Dathan, Abiram and 250 other leaders. They accused him of assuming his position. Moses' prayer in verse 15 was a pronouncement before the Lord of his refusal to abuse his leadership. Moses prayed, God did the terminating. Verses 31-35 states, *"Now it came to pass, as he finished speaking all these words, that the ground split apart under them, and the earth opened its mouth and swallowed them up, with their households and all the men with Korah, with all their goods..."* As sinkholes become more prevalent, note those who are swallowed, *"...So they and all those with them went down alive into the pit; the earth closed over them, and they perished from among the assembly. Then all Israel who were around them fled at their cry, for they said, 'Lest the earth swallow us up also!' And a fire came out from the LORD and consumed the two hundred and fifty men who were offering incense."* Whenever the nation was threatened by evildoers in their midst, Moses rose to the occasion and he brought the terminating Hand of God on the perpetrators. This scripture passage is an Old Testament picture of the apostolic authority we find in the New. After Herod killed James, Peter knew he was next! If we were in Peter's shoes, how would we pray? Had we been Peter, would we ask for an Ananias and Sapphira repeat? Paul and Barnabas probably brought this contribution in Acts 12 to the church in Jerusalem when James was killed and Peter's head was next on the chopping block. Acts 12:27-30 records Barnabus and Paul on assignment bringing financial relief to Jerusalem. They did not leave for home until Herod was dead and Peter was safe. The church prayed and as soon as Herod was in the grave, Barnabus and Paul had fulfilled their ministry and they were released to return to Antioch. How long will we remain enablers of evil by turning the other cheek when Layer 5 of God's love is the biblical answer for some who refuse to repent? By not stepping into this dimension, we continue to enable evil and we become responsible, in our generation, for the loss of harvest.

The prophet Zachariah was given a picture of the Throne-Room and how this process worked. Zachariah 6:9-13 states,

> *Then the word of the Lord came to me, saying: "Receive the gift from the captives – from Heldai, Tobijah, and Jedaiah, who have come from Babylon – and go the same day and enter the house of Josiah the son of Zephaniah. Take the silver and gold, make an elaborate crown, and set it on the head of Joshua the son of Jehozadak, the high priest. Then speak to him, saying, 'Thus says the Lord of hosts, saying: "Behold, the Man whose name is the BRANCH! From His place He shall branch out, And He shall build the temple of the Lord; Yes, He shall build the temple of the Lord. He shall bear the glory, And shall sit and rule on His throne; So He shall be a priest on His throne, And the counsel of peace shall be between them both."'"*

Jesus is the Branch, He rules on His Throne as a King and as a Priest. The counsel of peace is between the Kingly anointing and the Priestly anointing.

If there is no peace, and the church has none today over the condition of the nation, it is because we have not walked between the two. We have only used a Priestly anointing to offer people salvation. There is no fear of God in the land because there has been no manifestation of the Kingly anointing. When the King's judicial anointing is present, those who refuse to repent and continue destroying the land get terminated by God's Hand. That is God's love for the nation. It was love for the early church to terminate Ananias and Sapphira. This act saved monumental destruction. It was love that terminated Korah, Dathan, and Abiram and the two hundred and fifty leaders that wanted to end Moses' ministry. These acts of termination were acts of great mercy from our protective, vigilant Father, not the acts of a God of cruelty. Today, some proponents of perversion want to end the church's existence and jail believers who rise to speak against their perversity. Only God's judgment can save religious freedom. Either we embrace the Kingly or we lose cities and we lose nations. Today's church is nicer than God and that has to change. God is a Judge. He killed Ananias and Sapphira. He killed Korah, Dathan, Abiram and two hundred and fifty leaders, and in the book of Revelation at one point He kills one third of the population of the earth, while in another He kills a fourth. The Jesus you and I represent in the last days kills more people than He saves. That shows how difficult it will become to preach the Gospel. Unless we can ignore Romans 1 and remove the book of Revelation, we are confronted with the necessity for the anointing to terminate if we are going to have an end-time harvest. We will undoubtedly face radical opposition. Peter faced it with an anointing to terminate. Paul faced it with an anointing to afflict. Countless others throughout the centuries have walked in this anointing. Jesus has not changed. He is the same yesterday, today and forever. Will we find our counsel of peace between them both? Get to know Jesus the Judge! Walk with Him! He is real! He has not changed! He still afflicts and terminates!

In 2 Timothy 1:6-9 we find that Love Layer Five guarantees our destiny in Christ. It says,

> *Therefore I remind you to stir up the gift of God which is in you through the laying on of my hands. For God has not given us a spirit of fear, but of power and of love and of a sound mind. Therefore do not be ashamed of the testimony of our Lord, nor of me His prisoner, but share with me in the sufferings for the gospel according to the power of God, who has saved us and called us with a holy calling, not according to our works, but according to His own purpose and grace which was given to us in Christ Jesus before time began,...*

Our destiny was guaranteed before time began. The enemy often tries to cut that destiny short. He did it through Zipporah's reluctance to circumcise Moses' sons. Exodus 4:24-26 records the incident. *"And it came to pass on the way, at the encampment, that the Lord met him(Moses) and sought to kill him. Then Zipporah took a sharp stone and cut off the foreskin of her son and cast it at Moses' feet, and said, 'Surely you are a husband of blood to me!' So He let him go. Then she said, 'You are a husband of blood! – because of the circumcision.'"* God knew the death of the firstborn would ultimately free the Israelites who were connected by covenant. Moses' sons were outside the covenant until circumcised. The enemy warred against Paul and he warred against Peter. But God ensured their destiny. In order to ensure destiny, sometimes God has no other choice but to terminate.

One day the Lord asked me this, "Did I love you enough to send my own Son to die to save you?" I said, "Yes, Lord." He said, "Do I love you enough to put your enemies in the grave to preserve you?" It took me a little longer to answer that one, but the answer is the same. It is yes. Until the church spends as much time accepting the love of God that judges as receiving the love of God that saves we cannot fulfill our destiny! Without the Judicial Christ, we will always end up being enablers of evil. Without the Judicial Christ, we cannot find the counsel of peace. We have focused on one side of who God is in preference over the other. We have highlighted the Savior and practically ignored the Judge. That makes us lopsided and an enabler of evil rather than a confronter of it. Remember God's judicial love at its very core has the intent to save! He reluctantly terminates in order to save!

How does martyrdom fit with the Judicial Christ? Satan tried to take Jesus' life twice before He finished His race. Martyrdom is a call on the lives of many believers in the last days, but not before God's time!

Every time a Christian is martyred, the cry for judicial intervention grows stronger. Revelation 6:9-11 states,

> *When He opened the fifth seal, I saw under the altar the souls of those who had been slain for the word of God and for the testimony which they held. And they cried with a loud voice, saying, "How long, O Lord, holy and true, until You judge and avenge our blood on those who dwell on the earth?" Then a white robe was given to each of them; and it was said to them that they should rest a little while longer, until both the number of their fellow servants and their brethren, who would be killed as they were, was completed.*

The intercession of the martyrs changes from Priestly to Kingly in the last days. Both Jesus and Stephen forgave their torturers as Priestly examples. The Priestly Christ ruled at the beginning of the church age and the Kingly Christ rules at the end. Revelation 6:12-17 describes Kingly manifestations so great that kings and the rich hide in caves from God!

Who will represent the God from which they hide? The purpose for growing in the Kingly Christ is not to evade the call to martyrdom but to ensure that we go out on God's terms and not the devil's. The enemy tried to kill Jesus twice before His time. In Luke 4 at the beginning of His ministry preaching to His home town, they tried to throw Jesus off a hill but the Kingly Anointing manifested and everyone lost their grip! The second time was in John 8:59 but Jesus "*...hid Himself...*" and passed through them. Knowing the Kingly Christ allows us to finish our race and lay our life down on God's terms and not the enemy's! Reading the early church fathers is an eye-opener on martyrdom. They all voiced the expectations of martyrdom as their final great victory. Being denied martyrdom meant being cheated out of the better resurrection.

Paul finished his race and so can we! When we talk about the apostolic anointing to terminate, we must understand that its foundation has all been laid in the covenant of Sure Mercy. The covenant of Sure Mercy is the foundation of what Paul preached in Antioch and in Acts 13. It forms the foundation for the longest recorded message by the Apostle Paul in the entire New Testament. We are told in Acts 13:32-34, *"And we declare to you glad tidings – that promise which was made to the fathers. God has fulfilled this for us their children, in that He has raised up Jesus. As it is also written in the second Psalm: 'You are My Son, Today I have begotten You.' And that He raised Him from the dead, no more to return to corruption, He has spoken thus: 'I will give you the sure mercies of David.'"* Paul is preaching the covenant of Sure Mercy and telling us that Jesus guaranteed it to every single one of us. Now if Jesus guaranteed the covenant of Sure Mercy to us, the question is, what did He guarantee? Since it is the covenant of the Sure Mercies of David, we have to go back to 2 Samuel 7 where it was originally offered! (For a full treatment of this subject, see our book *The Sure Mercies of David*.)

In 2 Samuel 7:15,16 we are told, *"But My mercy shall not depart from him, as I took it from Saul, whom I removed from before you. And your house and your kingdom shall be established forever before you. Your throne shall be established forever."* God promised David that if he had a failure. God would not terminate him like He terminated Saul. The covenant of Sure Mercy promised an opportunity for mercy through repentance so that God could redeem failure and it would not utterly disqualify him, as it did Saul. David had a potentially disqualifying event with Bathsheba compounded by killing her husband, Uriah the Hittite. But because of his repentance, he did not lose his office, his call or his anointing. God redeemed his failure. Redemption for failure is what we are called to offer the world. Only those who rebelliously hang on to their sin to the point of destruction face the Judicial Hand of termination.

Termination was part of that covenant of Sure Mercy. Verses 8,9 of 2 Samuel 7 say, *"Now therefore, thus shall you say to My servant David, 'Thus says the LORD of hosts: "I took you from the sheepfold, from following the sheep, to be ruler over My people, over Israel. And I have been with you wherever you have gone, and have **cut off** all your enemies from before you, and have made you a great name, like the name of the great men who are on the earth."'"* Part of David's covenant of Sure Mercy was, "I will terminate all your enemies that refuse to relent." And God did. That is part of our covenant. The covenant promise of Sure Mercy was understood by the men who received it. If we want to understand the Davidic covenant that Jesus bought and paid for, all we have to do is go look at how David prayed his covenant in the Psalms. To use the Davidic covenant, we have to learn to pray like David prayed!

Psalm 5:6-10 reflects David's primary purpose in praying judicially. David presented facts in such a way as to move God toward a judicial decision. Psalm 5:1-10 says,

> *Give ear to my words, O Lord, Consider my meditation. Give heed to the voice of my cry, My King and my God, For to You I will pray. My voice You shall hear in the morning, O Lord; In the morning I will direct it to You, And I will look up. For You are not a God who takes pleasure in wickedness, Nor shall evil dwell with You. The boastful shall not stand in Your sight; You hate all workers of iniquity. You shall destroy those who speak falsehood; The Lord abhors the bloodthirsty and deceitful man. But as for me, I will come into Your house in the multitude of Your mercy; In fear of You I will worship toward Your holy temple. Lead me, O Lord, in Your righteousness because of my*

enemies; Make Your way straight before my face. For there is no faithfulness in their mouth; Their inward part is destruction; Their throat is an open tomb; They flatter with their tongue. Pronounce them guilty, O God! Let them fall by their own counsels; Cast them out in the multitude of their transgressions, For they have rebelled against You.

David demands termination for the guilty who rebel against God. The wicked wind up in the pit they create for the righteous! David again prayed for this level of termination in Psalm 7:8-16 for covenant justice when he said,

The Lord shall judge the peoples; Judge me, O Lord, according to my righteousness, And according to my integrity within me. Oh, let the wickedness of the wicked come to an end, But establish the just; For the righteous God tests the hearts and minds. My defense is of God, Who saves the upright in heart. God is a just judge, And God is angry with the wicked every day. If he does not turn back, He will sharpen His sword; He bends His bow and makes it ready. He also prepares for Himself instruments of death; He makes His arrows into fiery shafts. Behold, the wicked brings forth iniquity; Yes, he conceives trouble and brings forth falsehood. He made a pit and dug it out, And has fallen into the ditch which he made. His trouble shall return upon his own head, And his violent dealing shall come down on his own crown.

King David fought many enemies throughout his life but one thing was a sure foundation under his feet – the covenant of Sure Mercy that guaranteed God would "cut off" an unrelenting enemy. And Jesus guaranteed that same covenant to us. But where are we in that process personally? Do we realize that there is a mercy covenant that completely redeems failure? Covenant mercy qualifies us to pray judicially! The love of God that terminates is available so we can finish our race, fulfill our harvest and fulfill God's intent before the foundations of the earth. Love saves and love terminates. Until we grow into this understanding, we are simply enabling evil! It is time we grew into the fullness of Christ! The counsel of peace is between the Priestly and the Kingly! Jesus died to make us kings! Let's act like it!

Chapter 10

Apostolic Love in Judges

The word "*apostle*" is brought directly into English from Greek. Defining the word **ap-os-tol-os**, Kittle (the most complete etymological Greek dictionary) says, "In the first instances, this simply denotes the dispatch of a fleet (or army) or military or a military expedition...It then comes to be applied to the fleet itself and it thus acquires the meaning of a novel expedition...Meaning the Commander of an expedition e.g. the admiral."[ii] Many assignments from God qualify as novel expeditions! In the Old Testament, God appears to favor the Army in terminology, but in the New Testament His preference is clearly for the Navy!

The Old Testament book of Judges, perhaps more than any other, demonstrates the Layer of Love that is represented by the apostles. In Judges 1, seven of the twelve tribes have their failure specifically identified all with the same thread of refusing to completely eradicate the enemy as they were assigned. The problem is outlined by the words of the angel of the Lord who was sent before them to help them conquer the land. Judges 2:1-3 says,

> *Then the Angel of the LORD came up from Gilgal to Bochim, and said: "I led you up from Egypt and brought you to the land of which I swore to your fathers; and I said, 'I will never break My*

covenant with you. And you shall make no covenant with the inhabitants of this land; you shall tear down their altars.' But you have not obeyed My voice. Why have you done this? Therefore I also said, 'I will not drive them out before you; but they shall be thorns in your side, and their gods shall be a snare to you.'"

Israel's unsanctified mercy left people in place who would entice their hearts away from their One True God and ultimately destroy them. They did not obey the command of the Lord. When we refuse to enter into Love Layer Five, we empower the enemy. In Judges 1, those who, through unsanctified mercy, refused to bring the fullness of God's judgment ultimately ensured destruction on their nation and their land. As soon as Joshua's and the next generation were gone, Israel had generations that did not know war. They were in danger of losing all God had done for them. It may well be that the church today is in the same place. The seeker-sensitive model has produced huge churches where the congregations are fed biblical baby-food and are unaware of the spiritual war that rages! We desperately need a Joshua generation with a **heart for war**!

Judges 2:9-11 states of Joshua,

And they buried him within the border of his inheritance at Timnath Heres, in the mountains of Ephraim, on the north side of Mount Gaash. When all that generation had been gathered to their fathers, another generation arose after them who did not know the LORD nor the work which He had done for Israel. Then the children of Israel did evil in the sight of the LORD, and served the Baals;..."

As soon as the generations which warred for Israel's existence were gone, the following generations backslid and began to serve the false gods among them. This brought devastation and destruction.

Judges 3:1-4 describes the necessity of every generation learning how to war for their God-given freedoms. These verses state,

> *Now these are the nations which the LORD left, that He might test Israel by them, that is, all who had not known any of the wars in Canaan (this was only so that the generations of the children of Israel might be taught to know war, at least those who had not formerly known it), namely, five lords of the Philistines, all the Canaanites, the Sidonians, and the Hivites who dwelt in Mount Lebanon, from Mount Baal Hermon to the entrance of Hamath. And they were left, that He might test Israel by them, to know whether they would obey the commandments of the LORD, which He had commanded their fathers by the hand of Moses.*

Is this passage stunning to the modern mindset shaped mostly by "turn-the-other-cheek" love? God left vile people groups to see if Israel would destroy them. When the Israelites chose passivity, they lost their land. When the Israelites got in trouble and fell into judgment, the Spirit of God moved on an individual and he began to rise up and model the Jesus of Revelation 19:11. Revelation 19:11 says, *"Now I saw heaven opened, and behold, a white horse. And He who sat on him was called Faithful and True, and in righteousness He judges and makes war."* When we look at our New Testament apostles, we not only see them carrying a distinct message representing the Lord Jesus, but they also carried the authority of the Lord Jesus and could execute justice as needed for their mission. In this sense, they truly were like admirals of an expeditionary force. They had to judge and they had to war to establish their beachhead. They did it without hesitation and they did it because it was the assignment. When Israel was in deep distress from judgment for serving other gods, they began to cry out to the Living God. God's answer was a man of war with a judicial anointing. This individual used his anointing for war through the power of God and the enemy was subdued. Every believer, to navigate the volatility of the end-times, needs to know Jesus the Judge! Paul told the Galatians he labored until Christ was formed in them! I labor till Jesus the Judge is formed in you! God's judicial revelatory path for me started with *Purifying the Altar*, then *The Sure Mercies of David* followed by *Jesus and Justice*. The church needs to know the Judicial Christ.

Othniel was the first judge of Israel. Because of Othniel's willingness to judge evil and go to war, Israel was delivered and they had rest for forty years. This pattern begins to develop – when the children of Israel did evil in the sight of the Lord, they went into captivity. In Judges 3:12-14 we are told, *"And the children of Israel again did evil in the sight of the LORD. So the LORD strengthened Eglon king of Moab against Israel, because they had done evil in the sight of the LORD. Then he gathered to himself the people of Ammon and Amalek, went and defeated Israel, and took possession of the City of Palms. So the children of Israel served Eglon king of Moab eighteen years."* Has God strengthened our enemies? Israel's captivity would produce in the hearts of the people an intercessory heart-cry for deliverance. God then would release covenant love. It always followed the same pattern. Verses 15,16 state, *"But when the children of Israel cried out to the LORD, the LORD raised up a deliverer for them: Ehud the son of Gera, the Benjamite, a left-handed man. By him the children of Israel sent tribute to Eglon king of Moab. Now Ehud made himself a dagger (it was double-edged and a cubit in length) and fastened it under his clothes on his right thigh."* Covenant love manifested in a judicial anointing, the judge had to be willing to go to war. When that judge went to war, God showed up in behalf of His people and once again restored freedom to covenant Israel.

In Judges 4 we find that God is no respecter of persons and Deborah is called to be the first woman judge. Deborah prophetically spoke to Barak and said, "God is anointing you to go and deliver Israel." But Barak would not go without Deborah. They went together and again the enemy was destroyed and rest was restored to the land. God always answered the covenant cries of Israel by raising up a judge. That judge carried the authority of an admiral on an expedition to regain the freedom for the nation that God had intended. Jesus died for a harvest from every nation. The Judicial Jesus is the key to that harvest. He is the "Rod of Iron" that we are promised for subduing the resistance to our harvest.

The great thing about Gideon as a judge is that we see that God often uses the least of the least of the least. Gideon represented an individual who had to overcome his station in life to really answer the call because he never ever considered or thought he was qualified to be an admiral on a mission. When the angel of the Lord appeared to Gideon, his assessment in Judges 6:15 speaks to the sovereignty of God's Hand in choosing individuals. It says, *"So he said to Him, 'O my Lord, how can I save Israel? Indeed my clan is the weakest in Manasseh, and I am the least in my father's house.'"* Gideon was a member of the least tribe in Israel, Manasseh. His father was of the weakest clan in the tribe of Manasseh and he was the weakest in his father's house. If there was ever an individual who had to overcome a self-image problem, it was Gideon. He had three layers to battle through saying, "You cannot do this." His family, his clan and his tribe were completely unqualified. God forces us to choose identification either with our birth family or our spiritual family. In the restoration of apostolic authority to the church, we will probably have to fight the same battle that Gideon did when he was called. "Where I come from does not limit what I can do!" If Gideon failed, Israel continued in captivity. And so we find ourselves in such a place today. The restoration of apostolic authority in the church has a variety of purposes. One of those purposes is to avoid losing freedom by moving God's Judicial Hand on a defiling enemy and watching them be removed because of their refusal to repent. The only other option is an enemy growing stronger and stronger until captivity ensues.

An end-time church faces a rising antichrist spirit in their culture. This antichrist spirit promotes the kind of evil that demands judgment. The antichrist enemy works to completely destroy our harvest field through the promotion of evil. The shedding of innocent blood is enough to bring the destruction of any nation. We see it again and again in Scripture. Abortion qualifies as the shedding of innocent blood. The promotion of homosexuality demands the same penalty as shedding innocent blood! When the church supports political candidates and votes for people who openly promote what God abhors, we enable the destruction of various nations. How can we justify voting for those whose policies guarantee the destruction of our own cities? God discriminates against sin. He judges it and He brings destruction to both the perpetrators and those who support it. Anything less is forfeiting the apostolic call and the love that would restore freedom to the land. For this purpose, the Son of God was manifested, that He might destroy the works of the devil. Love destroys the wicked before their wickedness destroys the land!

Gideon had to learn war, but he was given unusual instruments, neither sword nor spear. He was given a pitcher, a torch and a word to shout. The word he shouted brought God into the midst and turned the enemies' swords on one another until they were destroyed. The vessel that contained the fire and light had to be broken. Like Gideon, when we go to war today, we go with the Word of the Lord on our lips and a Davidic intercession in our mouth. We go under the unction and direction of the Holy Spirit. We pray the Hand of God on the enemy – to convict them, to turn them and if they refuse to repent, to utterly erase their memory from the earth. Gideon was the perfect picture of the apostolic anointing when given to shoulder divine authority and walk out an appointed mission in obedience.

In Judges 8, Gideon was weak and weary from the battle and he asked the men of Succoth for provision. The men of Succoth answered Gideon in verses 6,7 saying, *"And the leaders of Succoth said, 'Are the hands of Zebah and Zalmunna now in your hand, that we should give bread to your army?' So Gideon said, 'For this cause, when the LORD has delivered Zebah and Zalmunna into my hand, then I will tear your flesh with the thorns of the wilderness and with briers!'"* They refused Gideon in his time of need. But God sustained Gideon and gave him victory. Verses 15,16 say, *"Then he came to the men of Succoth and said, 'Here are Zebah and Zalmunna, about whom you ridiculed me, saying, "Are the hands of Zebah and Zalmunna now in your hand, that we should give bread to your weary men?"' And he took the elders of the city, and thorns of the wilderness and briers, and with them he taught the men of Succoth."* Apostolic anointing carries with it the ability to teach by declaring and releasing affliction. Part of God's judicial armory has adversity in it that can be released as needed. When misguided politicians and Supreme Court justices arrogantly support evil, they deserve the heavy Hand of God! Apostolic authority moves that Hand! Apostolic authority has to be restored to the church.

Perhaps the most interesting verse in Judges is 8:21. It says, *"So Zebah and Zalmunna said, 'Rise yourself, and kill us; for as a man is, so is his strength.' So Gideon arose and killed Zebah and Zalmunna, and took the crescent ornaments that were on their camels' necks."* When Gideon destroyed Zebah and Zalmunna, he took from their camels crescent ornaments. There is one religion today which uses a crescent ornament. With the emergence of the apostolic anointing comes the authority to move the Judicial Hand of God and subdue those who would shed innocent blood. Hebrews 11 challenges us to use our faith in this realm. God has apostolic authority for the church. The question is, are we going to receive it and will we grow in it until it can be fully released against the enemies of Christ? The love of God to Israel manifested through the judges brought death to the promoters of evil so that freedom could be restored. Did God love us enough to send His own Son to save us? We can say yes to that!

That becomes a foundation for the next question. If God loved us enough to send His own Son to save us, does He not love us enough to kill those who are intent on destroying our life and ministry? The Bible answers that clearly. God absolutely loves us enough to kill those who are intent on destroying our lives and our ministries. Is there any parent who would not pull the trigger if a serial killer threatened their children? Yet we have Christians who hesitate to pull the prayer-trigger against serial-abortion-promoting politicians. Apostolic love means standing up in our God-given authority and through prayer moving the Judicial Hand of God on the enemy and bringing deliverance. When the people cried out for deliverance, every enemy in the book of Judges died at the hand of the anointed judge. When an anointed judge stood in concert with the Ultimate Anointed Judge, enemies died. The consistent message of the book of Judges is that God gives the authority to subdue our enemies and restore our covenantal freedom. When the church today realizes that restoring apostolic authority means releasing the anointing of the judges, then I believe we are going to see Samuels arise who choose morality, holiness and the character of Christ. Because they choose the character of Christ, the Judge of all the Earth walks with them every step of the way. Perhaps the greatest way to prepare for the restoration of the apostolic anointing is to spend time in the book of Judges and get to know the covenantal Savior who delivers by an anointing to war. God killed for Israel's judges. What will God do when we pray His Spirit-anointed prayers? Luke 17:29 in the 1984 NIV says, *"But the day Lot left Sodom, fire and sulfur rained down from heaven and destroyed them all."* What happens when we leave town? In 1 Samuel 16:4, Samuel came to Bethlehem and the elders trembled in fear that he was not coming in peace! It seems like the witnesses of Revelation would generate some fear! We know there is an appointed season for the Judicial Christ to prevail! Will God give us a measure of that anointing to bring in a harvest of nations? God gave it in Acts and the prophets imply a double for the last days! Joel 2:23-29 declares,

> *Be glad then, you children of Zion, And rejoice in the Lord your God; For He has given you the former rain faithfully, And He will cause the rain to come down for you – The former rain, And the latter rain in the first month. The threshing floors shall be full of wheat, And the vats shall overflow with new wine and oil. "So I will restore to you the years that the swarming locust has eaten, The crawling locust, The consuming locust, And the chewing locust, My great army which I sent among you. You shall eat in plenty and be satisfied, And praise the name of the Lord your God, Who has dealt wondrously with you; And My people shall never be put to shame. Then you shall know that I am in the midst of Israel: I am the Lord your God And there is no other. My people shall never be put to shame. "And it shall come to pass afterward That I will pour out My Spirit on all flesh; Your sons and your daughters shall prophesy, Your old men shall dream dreams, Your young men shall see visions. And also on My menservants and on My maidservants I will pour out My Spirit in those days.*

Representing the Judicial Christ opens the door to a harvest of nations!

Chapter 11

The Power to Resist

Christians have selectively lost freedoms previous generations bled and died for because the church resembles castrated calves. Matthew 5:38-39 taken out of context is the knife that has neutered the church, *"You have heard that it was said, 'An eye for an eye and a tooth for a tooth.' But I tell you not to resist an evil person. But whoever slaps you on your right cheek, turn the other to him also."* In the book of Revelation, Jesus demonstrates love that resists from His ascended Throne by threatening to remove the wicked! The book of Revelation promises plagues for rebellious nations. Love is multi-faceted and not one dimensional. Love has more than one response. Walking in the Spirit means finding God's appropriate level of either compassion or resistance, and embracing it in prayer! The Jesus of Revelation destroys more than He saves! The current condition of our culture lends understanding to why Jesus is so judicial in the book of Revelation! Indeed, many political and spiritual leaders spit in the Lord's face by condoning lifestyles which God declares will keep us from His kingdom.

1 Peter 5:6-9 tells us, *"Therefore humble yourselves under the mighty hand of God, that He may exalt you in due time, casting all your care upon Him, for He cares for you. Be sober, be vigilant; because your adversary the devil walks about like a roaring lion, seeking whom he may devour.* **Resist** *him, steadfast in the faith, knowing that the same sufferings are experienced by your brotherhood in the world."* The word

for 'resist' in verse 9 is **anth-his-tay-mee**, the same word used in Matthew 5:39 According to Peter we are commanded to resist the enemy and dislodge him from his position. James 4:6-8 says, *"But He gives more grace. Therefore He says: 'God resists the proud, But gives grace to the humble.' Therefore submit to God.* **Resist** *the devil and he will flee from you. Draw near to God and He will draw near to you. Cleanse your hands, you sinners; and purify your hearts, you double-minded."* James' view also is that we are commanded to resist the enemy.

Now, if we were dishonest interpreters of the Word, we could say "So far it is two against one. Both Peter and James command us to resist while Jesus commands us not to resist." Resolving seeming discrepancies in Scripture requires honesty, openness and a willingness to adjust and modify cherished traditions because Jesus said the Scripture cannot be broken! Jesus identified one circumstance where we are not to resist while James and Peter command us to resist! How do we resolve the seeming conflict? The problem is, the men who Jesus trained also reflected His views. Jesus trained them to resist. Jesus took a stance in the temple both at the beginning of His ministry and at the end of His ministry by resisting in very similar encounters. The Holy Spirit led the early church to resist governmental commands to be silent. They resisted the threats of the Sanhedrin. They resisted evil at every opportunity. The early church resolved the conflict between obeying God or bowing to government. They obeyed God and prayed judgment on government! They developed saints of strength, courage and boldness who had no problem resisting. What are we developing today? Are we developing enablers of evil because we have misunderstood and misrepresented God's love?

There are two very strong responses by Paul when he was confronted by evil. As radically as Jesus resisted evil in the temple, so did Paul when his destiny was challenged. Paul did not readily "turn-the-other-cheek." There are two places where the Apostle Paul finds himself being resisted by demonically-inspired individuals. In 2 Timothy 4:14,15 we read, *"Alexander the coppersmith did me much harm. May the Lord repay him according to his works. You also must beware of him, for he has greatly **resisted** our words."* Alexander the coppersmith was dead-set against Paul and his ministry. As a result Paul prayed a judicial prayer that was definitive. He asked God's judgment on Alexander to parallel his actions. Paul's prayer turned Alexander's adversarial actions on his own head. Evil people dig a pit and God pushes them into the very pit they dig. Evil Haman in the book of Esther constructed a gallows. Haman's determination to kill the Jews got him hung on the very gallows he constructed. God's love for His covenant people killed Haman! "...*Repay him according to his works*" speaks to the entirety of God's justice as it was meted out in the Bible, in both Old and New Testaments. There is no "turn-the-other-cheek" in Paul on this issue. When Paul was facing serious resistance from a false prophet, Matthew 5 "turn-the-other-cheek" would have forfeited a harvest. How many of God's intended harvests have we forfeited? Can we begin to see why Jesus would say, "My church looks like castrated calves"? Until we can pray and move God's Hand to turn the plans and purposes of God's enemies on their own heads, we have not grown to parallel the early church! Herod killed James and seeing it pleased the Jews. Herod intended the same for Peter. Constant prayer was made for Peter. The results have to reflect the nature of the prayers. An angel was dispatched to get Peter out of jail. An angel ended Herod's life! Where are the prayers that cause angelic intervention. Surely we can pray evil politician's plans on their own heads!

In Acts 13 when the false prophet, demonically empowered, stood against Paul, Paul did not turn the other cheek. We are told in Acts 13:8, *"But Elymas the sorcerer (for so his name is translated)*

withstood/anth-his-tay-mee *them, seeking to turn the proconsul away from the faith."* Elymas projected demonic **anth-his-tay-mee** against Paul. What was Paul's response when he encountered this kind of conflict? He brought the Judicial Hand of God and blindness on the false prophet. If I were to imagine the opposite of "turn-the-other-cheek" then what Paul did in this passage must be close! Not only did Paul actively resist the agent of evil but his prayers brought a devastating display of God's Judicial Hand. The false prophet had to wander around in blindness, not seeing the sun. It was very effective. The amazing fruit was that the proconsul believed. Where is the Jesus who loves like this today? Can we find Him in church? Can we find Him in today's seminaries? Most of our seminaries have become breeding grounds for passivity and sites for spiritual castration. We have very few seminaries that teach balanced Biblical resistance! Our seminaries teach love that is passive. We should teach judicial love but very few have paid the price to walk in this realm. The trail was blazed by the early church and the Spirit bids us walk in their steps! If our paradigm only allows "turn-the-other-cheek" then we have misunderstood the Lord, taken Scripture out of context and are doomed to spiritual dullness that makes us appear to Jesus like castrated calves.

How did we get so passive? The Lord challenged me to search church history to see what it was like to go to church a hundred years ago in America. One account is descriptive of the strong walk we once saw among church leaders. In September of 1901, Mordecai Ham Jr. preached from the pulpit his grandfather had occupied for forty years and the Holy Spirit moved. He entered the ministry that day and became a fearless representative of both Jesus the Savior and Jesus the Judge. On page 32 of Edward E. Ham's biography, *50 Years on the Battle Front with Christ*, we find this account illustrating Mordecai Ham's courage and convictions:

On that second night it seemed all 'hell' broke loose as the moonshine crowd stole up around the church, after we had begun the meeting, and threw rocks at us. They unharnessed the horses, cut the saddle straps and stole everything they could carry off." Ham went out and confronted the ringleader, who proceeded to pull a knife on him. "Put up that knife, you coward. If you were not a coward you wouldn't pull a knife on an unarmed man. Now I'm going to ask the Lord either to convert you and your crowd or to kill you." "Do as you damn please," he snarled at me as he stalked off. I prayed, and that bully was dying the next morning. They called for me to go and pray for him, but he died before I got to his bedside. On that same day a neighborhood saw mill blew up and killed three others of the crowd. That night I announced from the pulpit that I wanted everything that had been stolen the preceding evening brought to the church on the next night and that the Lord might kill any person who tried to keep something that didn't belong to him. Twenty–four hours later I took inventory and announced that we would pray because one saddle was still missing. Some fellow in the congregation jumped up and hollered, "You needn't pray; it will be here in a few minutes." And it was.[iii]

Mordecai Ham, the man who won Billy Graham to Jesus was proficient in love layer five. The biblical record testifies to the multiple dimensions of God's love! Not one of the early apostles conducted his life and ministry in a way that fit the primary concept of love in today's church. That should tell us that Matthew 5 has been used by the enemy to weaken the church. Jesus in Matthew 4 was tempted with the same ploy. Jesus was spiritually astute enough to recognize the origin. We have been hoodwinked!

The Lord took me to Matthew 4, and He broadened my understanding of verse 5. Matthew 4:5 says, *"Then the devil took Him up into the holy city, set Him on the pinnacle of the temple,…"* The Lord said, "I want you to notice that satan took Jesus to 'church.'" I recognized that Jesus was giving me a new way to view this Scripture. Then He said, "Notice what happened next in verse 6, '*…and said to Him, "If You are the Son of God, throw Yourself down. For it is written: 'He shall give His angels charge over you,' and, 'In their hands they shall bear you up, Lest you dash your foot against a stone.'"* Satan preached Jesus a message." The devil took Jesus to church and then preached Him a message. And it was not just any message from some out-of-the-way, obscure Scripture that nobody knew. This message came out of a familiar Psalm of protection: Psalm 91. What was the temptation? The enemy took the Scripture out of context in order to entice Jesus into presumption. The devil took Jesus to church and preached Him a message.

We have to ask ourselves: what was satan's original job? According to Ezekiel he was a worship leader in heaven. His job as worship leader meant he spent much time in church. Satan knows the Word. The point is, the devil has taken us to church and preached us a message over and over and over again, until love displayed in the New Testament has been redefined one-dimensionally. Satan has defined love as "Do not resist an evil person, but 'turn-the-other-cheek' and pray for them." If "turn-the-other-cheek" and "do-not-resist-evil" dominates our view of Christlikeness, we have lost the battle and become enablers of evil. Peter, James, John and Paul all found themselves in situations which required different layers of God's love that necessitated resistance. The enemy has tried to convince us that the definition of God's love is pure kindness and mercy even to the point of not resisting evil. This successful ruse has enabled him over the last fifty years to steal freedoms that generations of Christians died to birth. Having a limited and skewed definition of love has been very costly. We need Ananias and Sapphira events in our courtrooms and among the decision-makers of our nations. God's Hand of affliction or termination is appropriate in many legislative arenas! Learning to love the way God does transforms our prayer lives. Let God arise and His enemies be scattered!

Why does Revelation portray Jesus as both 'Afflicter in Chief' and 'Terminator in Chief'? Because there have always been people more committed to their sin than desirous of accepting a Savior. Those who make God illegal in the public square via hate-speech laws demonstrate an antichrist spirit that demands judicial intervention! God discriminates against sin by judging those who promote it! If we vote for politicians who belong to political parties that promote it, then we participate in their sin and consequently in their judgment!

The New Testament as a whole teaches that God's love responds in varying degrees determined by the depth of evil we face and the guidance of the Holy Spirit. "Turn-the-other-cheek" has become a "one-size-fits-all' imbalanced definition of love! The early church did more resisting than they did turning the cheek. Why has it become our sole definition of love? Who benefits from this definition? The fruit of this theology is passivity where most of the church with a once vibrant testimony for the Living God has been transformed into an enabler of evil. Segments of the church now condone that which violates Scripture. Denominations are, in some instances, ordaining homosexual priests and are guilty of enabling evil. Apostasy has become the fruit of love that turns-the-cheek. It is time for the church to regain its authority. God's love has a mature structure with breadth, length, width and depth. Walking in mature, Kingly love will bring God's power on the scene in judicial manifestation. Let politicians beware –

do not promote what God hates and force the church to ask Jesus to visit you!

Jesus loved sinners by turning the other cheek. But He also loved by warning, afflicting and even terminating. God's love always has the goal of saving people and bringing in a harvest. While we accept and love sinners, divine love does not, in wisdom, open arms and doors to those who glory and revel in their sin. God's love manifests in five different ways each specific to the situation and the individual. We are called to represent both the Savior and the Judge. We must learn how to pray in order to love as He loves! Here is a condensed chart of each layer's purpose and the five-fold gifting it corresponds to, a brief guide to God's Layered Love. When representing the Priestly Savior, we pray **for** people, but a shift comes when representing the King because now we become agents that pray **against** those intent on destruction. May our prayers carry the weight of the Throne we represent!

God's Layered Love

Layer of Love	Five-fold gifting	New Testament Examples	Explanation
Acceptance	Evangelist	Jesus dining with Zacchaeus Jesus dining with publicans and sinners Mat 5:39 Do not resist an evil person	Evangelists love the lost into truth through their ability to overlook evil. Their love-expression for the lost manifests as unconditional acceptance. That love can be so great often they overlook sin and, in kindness, love a person into the Kingdom. The evangelist is empowered to turn the other cheek and pray for his enemies. This is a foundational piece of God's Heart — one the evangelist must help impart to the whole body of Christ! In the evangelistic mode, we do not resist an evil person but manifest God's love through acceptance.
Forbearance	Pastor	2 Pet 3:9 The Lord is longsuffering, not willing that any perish Jesus' refusal to condemn adulteress	Love allows time for trial, error, growth and redemption. Pastoral forbearance covers us while we mature enough to recognize our need for personal transformation and change. God is long-suffering concerning our failures in the hope of repentance and restoration. Pastoral love demonstrates God's forbearance toward us as God gives us time and space to pound out the crooked places, apply spot remover and deal with the blemishes that are inherent in all the missteps and adversity that our souls endure as we develop on the earth. Forbearance has an eternal purpose — always to bring about the acknowledgment of sin and ultimately, specific true repentance! As leaders our forbearance facilitates a safe place for growth!
Warning	Prophet	Mat. 3:7-12 John the Baptist warning people: "Repent!..." Col. 1:28 Paul instructs us to warn every man	Jesus dramatically resisted evil when moving as a prophet. And it is the prophet's job to love purity and love people by warning them when in violation. The Greek word for 'admonish' is nou-thet-eh-o, which is the same Greek word for 'warning'. Warning, in Scripture, has a very distinctive purpose. Those who never cultivate friends who speak hard truth will have a very difficult time growing into fullness. The piece of the resurrected Christ that prophets represent purposes to save people from adversity. When Paul wrote 1 Corinthians, he moved prophetically in warning and the purpose was saving God's people from affliction. Warning is a dimension of God's love that we need to understand and embrace in expressing God's kingdom love.
Affliction	Teacher	Alexander the Coppersmith Paul's blindness on the road to Damascus Hebrews 12:5-9 James 3:1-:2	In Colossians 1, Paul makes it clear that it is impossible to grow people to fullness, maturity and completion without also teaching every man. God intervenes in the lives of people in order to correct mistakes, curb passions and instruct in virtue. Chastening is used primarily to amend behavior. It causes us to change how we think and how we act. Teaching provides building blocks toward maturity, and often affliction is the only way people will turn from sin. John the Baptist promised a Savior who would baptize with the Holy Spirit and fire! The baptism of fire seems to be affliction aimed at burning up the hindrances in our life that are obstructing God's eternal purposes! While we may hate the process, it produces the eternal fruit of Christlikeness!
Termination	Apostle	Acts 5:1-11 Ananias and Sapphira Acts 12:20-23 Herod's encounter with worms	Those who steadfastly, consistently resist God reach a point over time where their continued rebellion fills a cup of iniquity. When the cup is full, a process leading to judgment is initiated. The reason God judges, the reason He wars, the reason He terminates is because there are purveyors of evil who refuse to repent and who are determined to destroy our God-given harvest field. One aspect of the apostolic call was terminating the resistance when the rebellious refused to release their evil assignment. Those who stand in opposition to God's purpose and plan face a determined Judge! Love through apostolic authority is demonstrated by prayer that releases angels who terminate, just as Ananias and Sapphira and Herod were terminated. Love purposes to save and Apostolic love saves by cutting off agents of evil.

Chapter 12

Understanding Judicial Love

One of the reasons that "turn-the-other-cheek" is so easy to take out of context is its placement at the beginning of the longest recorded message that Jesus ever gave. Jesus was preparing the Twelve and later the Seventy to be sent out as evangelists. The conclusion to the instructions and preparation for sending does not appear until Matthew 10 where Jesus balanced "turn-the-other-cheek" with a prophetic, judicial, covenantal judgment on those who refused the message. In Christ we are Abraham's seed and heirs according to the promise. Abraham's covenant had two options: those who bless you, I will bless, those who curse you, I will curse. That principle continues in Matthew 10:14,15, *"And whoever will not receive you nor hear your words, when you depart from that house or city, shake off the dust from your feet. Assuredly, I say to you, it will be more tolerable for the land of Sodom and Gomorrah in the day of judgment than for that city!"* Jesus finally concludes what it means to be mature as your Heavenly Father is mature. Maturity judges the rejection of the message and invokes biblical judgment on the rejecters in order to hopefully save the city. Shaking the dust off their feet was declaring a biblical covenantal judgment. Why have we abandoned Jesus' ways for a compromised gospel? Love warned of coming judgment on the unrepentant in the hope of **saving them**. Love warns and occasionally love acts judicially in order to arrest evil before it completely destroys a culture.

In Luke 10 where Jesus sent out the Seventy, the clarity over this principle solidifies as He instructs them. Luke 10:1-12 states,

> *After these things the Lord appointed seventy others also, and sent them two by two before His face into every city and place where He Himself was about to go. Then He said to them, "The harvest truly is great, but the laborers are few; therefore pray the Lord of the harvest to send out laborers into His harvest. Go your way; behold, I send you out as lambs among wolves. Carry neither money bag, knapsack, nor sandals; and greet no one along the road. But whatever house you enter, first say, 'Peace to this house.' And if a son of peace is there, your peace will rest on it; if not, it will return to you. And remain in the same house, eating and drinking such things as they give, for the laborer is worthy of his wages. Do not go from house to house. Whatever city you enter, and they receive you, eat such things as are set before you. And heal the sick there, and say to them, 'The kingdom of God has come near to you.' But whatever city you enter, and they do not receive you, go out into its streets and say, 'The very dust of your city which clings to us we wipe off against you. Nevertheless know this, that the kingdom of God has come near you.' But I say to you that it will be more tolerable in that Day for Sodom than for that city.*

Jesus commanded the Seventy to invoke a covenantal judgment on any city that rejected the Word. What happened to "turn-the-other-cheek" and "pray-for-your-enemies"? Rejecters of the Word were warned of eternal, fiery judgment!

In the exhortation to the Seventy, Jesus made it clear that they were to go out into the streets, shake the dust off their feet and declare in front of everybody that judgment for that city would be worse than what Sodom and Gomorrah endured. It seems in opposition to

Matthew 5:38 "turn-the-other-cheek," but in fact it greatly augments it! This passage is really strong! We need to realize that Jesus included in His preparational marching orders, for the Twelve in Matthew 10 and the Seventy in Luke 10, consequences that dropped a severe eternal plumbline. Tradition has excised this part of Christ's preparation to foster spiritual passivity. Jesus was anything but passive! When He faced evil in the temple, He acted. When He sent the Twelve and the Seventy out, He was very clear with them: When your message is not received, you invoke a judicial covenantal warning, obviously in the hope that people would hear it and decide to change. Jesus made it clear that in the evangelistic mode, "turn-the-other-cheek" only lasts for a period then follows warning about coming judgment. How long were they to "turn-the-other-cheek"? This question has to be answered! Jesus is a reluctant Judge and when He acts, it is always to accomplish salvation. The Holy Spirit knows how long to wait for salvation before moving to the next dimension of love. When we love the way God loves, we transition with the Spirit of God. "Turn-the-other-cheek" predominated while they were evangelizing, but once released if they were not received, they pronounced judgment and departed for the next city. What seminary teaches our ministers how to walk with Jesus the Judge? What seminary teaches disciples to shake the dust off their feet? May this be a training manual for just such preparation! The disciples received their baptism of fire by being with Jesus when He cleaned house in the Temple! Until we sign on to represent the Judicial Christ, we are only selectively walking in His footsteps! The early church volunteered to be martyred for the truth. How does this compare with our generation of believers who can barely utter an oppositional word? What would the early Church Fathers have said to abortion or ordaining homosexual priests? The early church would have prayed, declared and decreed God's Judicial Hand. Rome disintegrated under the weight of moral corruption! But not before the Gospel was spread into many nations by believing, God-fearing priests!

The early church established the doctrine of the Trinity affirming the equality of the Father, Son and Holy Spirit as co-equal and co-eternal. A leader named Arias disagreed, declaring the superiority of the Father. The Council of Nicea was convened to settle this issue! The Council of Nicea rejected Arius' doctrine. Arius had a contingency plan, which resulted in the emperor demanding that he be restored to his position:

> Arius, after Nicea, regained power through political influences. On Arias' recall, Alexander, Primate of Alexandria, in tears prostrated himself in the sacrarium, praying, "If Arius comes tomorrow to the church, take me away, and let me not perish with the guilty. But if Thou pittiest Thy Church, as Thou dost pity it, take Arius away, lest when he enters heresy enter with him." The next morning, on his triumphant procession to the church to be formally and publicly reconciled on imperial authority, Arius stopped and left the procession suddenly because of gastric pain. After waiting some time, his followers investigated and found that the old man Arius had collapsed in blood and fallen headlong into the open latrine. The orthodox party triumphantly recalled the words concerning Judas' death, who "falling headlong, burst asunder in the midst" and died (Acts 1:18). Arius' manner of death was used by the orthodox to discomfit the heretics and encourage the saints, and it was declared an act of God. The heretics preferred to forget it, and modern heretics have eliminated this and like events from history books as "irrelevant." It was, however, a providential conclusion to the great intellectual and spiritual battle of Nicea.[iv]

God answered the prayer of a priest. The answer to that prayer presents a picture of the New Testament Judicial Christ. The heretic took a fatal nosedive into an open latrine. May today's church see equally specific answers to prayer!

A Catholic priest prayed judicially and God answered! Throughout church history, God has answered prayers and intervened to save His church! The prayer book of the Bible is the Psalms. Every Christian can pray Psalm 5:4-10 over our judges, politicians, educators and some ministers. Doing anything less in this hour could contribute to the passivity that loses nations. Psalm 5:4-10 states,

> *For You are not a God who takes pleasure in wickedness, Nor shall evil dwell with You. The boastful shall not stand in Your sight; You hate all workers of iniquity. You shall destroy those who speak falsehood; The Lord abhors the bloodthirsty and deceitful man. But as for me, I will come into Your house in the multitude of Your mercy; In fear of You I will worship toward Your holy temple. Lead me, O Lord, in Your righteousness because of my enemies; Make Your way straight before my face. For there is no faithfulness in their mouth; Their inward part is destruction; Their throat is an open tomb; They flatter with their tongue. Pronounce them guilty, O God! Let them fall by their own counsels; Cast them out in the multitude of their transgressions, For they have rebelled against You.*

How should believers respond to lying, deceiving politicians who say one thing to get elected and do the opposite once in office? Moses faced blatant, defiling, destructive sin for which the nation could have perished. On several occasions Moses was faced with an angry God ready to destroy the entire nation and each time Moses moved God's wrath from the nation to the much smaller group of perpetrators. Moses averted the loss of the nation by focusing justice on the perpetrators. Moses prayed justice on those defiling the nation and God removed them. Three thousand fell in one hour due to sexual sin, but the nation was saved. Praying the full weight of God's Judicial Throne on organizations and individuals who champion evil is the only way to avert terminal judgment on the nation! Praying termination on the perpetrators may stop termination of the nation. When this principle reoccurs multiple times, we have to take it seriously! Moses prayed this way as a shepherd to save the flock. God answered him consistently! Praying mercy on the nation sometimes means asking for those championing evil to be cut off! When God cuts off, He can remove by resignation, by disability, by loss of office, by hardship and ultimately by death. God can cut off the finances, cut off favor or cut off mental acuity. God cut off all David's enemies and Acts 13 states Jesus extends that covenant to us through His blood. God obligates Himself by covenant to cut off our enemies. Pray David's Psalms! Psalm 20:1-9 cries for what we seek,

> I will praise You, O Lord, with my whole heart; I will tell of all Your marvelous works. I will be glad and rejoice in You; I will sing praise to Your name, O Most High. When my enemies turn back, They shall fall and perish at Your presence. For You have maintained my right and my cause; You sat on the throne judging in righteousness. You have rebuked the nations, You have destroyed the wicked; You have blotted out their name forever and ever. O enemy, destructions are finished forever! And you have destroyed cities; Even their memory has perished. But the Lord shall endure forever; He has prepared His throne for judgment. He shall judge the world in righteousness, And He shall administer judgment for the peoples in uprightness. The Lord also will be a refuge for the oppressed, A refuge in times of trouble.

◆ God's Layered Love ◆

Chapter 13

Why does Love Terminate?

In Genesis 1, God created the heavens and the earth. He then created man, male and female, commanding them to populate the earth! By the time we reach Genesis 6, we discover that the creation had taken a decided turn toward evil. In Genesis 6:5-7 and 17,18 we are told,

> *Then the Lord saw that the wickedness of man was great in the earth, and that **every** intent of the thoughts of his heart was **only evil continually**. And the Lord was sorry that He had made man on the earth, and He was grieved in His heart. So the Lord said, "I will destroy man whom I have created from the face of the earth, both man and beast, creeping thing and birds of the air, for I am sorry that I have made them... And behold, I Myself am bringing floodwaters on the earth, to destroy from under heaven all flesh in which is the breath of life; everything that is on the earth shall die. But I will establish My covenant with you; and you shall go into the ark – you, your sons, your wife, and your sons' wives with you."*

Why did love destroy? Because rather than see wickedness rule the creation, God intervened and established boundaries for evil. God's judgments are boundaries so that evil can no longer completely and totally prevail in the earth. Without the loving judgments of God, evil would prevail.

Evil begins to prevail when the church neglects their assignment to be courageous and vigilant to declare and call into existence God's judgment against those who practice evil. If tenured judges practice evil, they should encounter the Judicial Christ! Praying the Judicial Hand of God on the wicked is a saving work. In the flood of Genesis 6, it has been estimated by Tom Pickett that over the 1656 years from Creation to the flood a reasonable population would be between 5 and 17 billion with an average of 10 billion. If God did not hesitate to destroy ten billion people over wickedness, what should we expect in the days ahead? Since Matthew 24:37 says, *"As it was in the days of Noah, so it will be at the coming of the Son of man,"* can we expect judicial manifestations in an attempt to arrest evil? Love judges evil workers who refuse to repent! Love terminates when absolutely necessary!

Genesis 19, which describes Sodom, focuses on a loving intervention to stop the spread of evil. Another passage referring to Sodom, Ezekiel 16:49,50, adds the adjectives, arrogant, haughty, unconcerned, overfed and refusing to help the poor or needy. Termination, in Noah's time, was ultimately about salvation, not destruction. Genesis 19:23-25 describes the loving intervention of God establishing a boundary against evil. It says, *"The sun had risen upon the earth when Lot entered Zoar. Then the Lord rained brimstone and fire on Sodom and Gomorrah, from the Lord out of the heavens. So He overthrew those cities, all the plain, all the inhabitants of the cities, and what grew on the ground."* Current excavations indicate the population of Sodom and Gomorrah and the surrounding plain was around 3,000,000 people.

The New Testament book of Jude makes clear that God's loving purpose of intervening with judgments has not changed. Jude 5-7 states,

> *But I want to remind you, though you once knew this, that the Lord, having saved the people out of the land of Egypt, afterward destroyed those who did not believe. And the angels who did not keep their proper domain, but left their own abode, He has reserved in everlasting chains under darkness for the judgment of the great day; as Sodom and Gomorrah, and the cities around them in a similar manner to these, having given themselves over to sexual immorality and gone after strange flesh, are set forth as an example, suffering the vengeance of eternal fire.*

Will God overthrow a nation because some states choose to promote sexual immortality? Will God overthrow a military because they allow and support perversion? Will the love of God once again bring the vengeance of eternal fire?

The answer is yes, according to 2 Peter 3:7-10 which states,

> *But the heavens and the earth which are now preserved by the same word, are reserved for fire until the day of judgment and perdition of ungodly men. But, beloved, do not forget this one thing, that with the Lord one day is as a thousand years, and a thousand years as one day. The Lord is not slack concerning His promise, as some count slackness, but is longsuffering toward us, not willing that any should perish but that all should come to repentance. But the day of the Lord will come as a thief in the night, in which the heavens will pass away with a great noise, and the elements will melt with fervent heat; both the earth and the works that are in it will be burned up.*

One thing is consistent from Genesis to Revelation: the love of God does intervene with judgments. When He intervenes with fire, a new heavens and earth, in which righteousness dwells, will be birthed! And the wicked will have no place there. Most of us have been given a view of love where **everyone** gets mercy. More times than not, mercy to the righteous means removal of the wicked! Heaven is open to judicial prayer for the removal of wicked leaders. Do we know the God who terminates?

Genesis 38:6,7 says, *"Then Judah took a wife for Er his firstborn, and her name was Tamar. But Er, Judah's firstborn, was wicked in the sight of the Lord, and the Lord killed him."* Love intervenes when a person's heart is set on wickedness and God removes them before they can damage their generation.

Verses 8-10 state,

And Judah said to Onan, "Go in to your brother's wife and marry her, and raise up an heir to your brother." But Onan knew that the heir would not be his; and it came to pass, when he went in to his brother's wife, that he emitted on the ground, lest he should give an heir to his brother. And the thing which he did displeased the Lord; therefore He killed him also.

This passage demonstrates how invested God is in populating the earth. Refusing to participate with God in creation was, in this instance, something God judged worthy of death. It has certainly never risen to that level over my lifetime, but perhaps we do not realize how important creation is to God, and the part we have to play in that process. In Exodus 1:22 we are told, *"So Pharaoh commanded all his people, saying, 'Every son who is born you shall cast into the river, and every daughter you shall save alive.'"* Because Pharaoh sought to destroy the Deliverer, he ordered the death of many male children! Eighty years later, judgment came!

Exodus 12:29 says, "*And it came to pass at midnight that the Lord struck all the firstborn in the land of Egypt, from the firstborn of Pharaoh who sat on his throne to the firstborn of the captive who was in the dungeon, and all the firstborn of livestock.*" God's loving judgment intervened in Egypt, to set the Israelites free. What would California look like if God intervened to set the church free? In Exodus 32:10 we are told, "*Now therefore, let Me alone, that My wrath may burn hot against them and I may consume them. And I will make of you a great nation.*" God was ready to destroy the entire Israelite nation because of their idolatry and start over with Moses. But Moses interceded for the nation and in order to spare it, the perpetrators had to suffer judgment.

Exodus 32:25-28 states,

> *Now when Moses saw that the people were unrestrained (for Aaron had not restrained them, to their shame among their enemies), then Moses stood in the entrance of the camp, and said, "Whoever is on the Lord's side – come to me!" And all the sons of Levi gathered themselves together to him. And he said to them, "Thus says the Lord God of Israel: 'Let every man put his sword on his side, and go in and out from entrance to entrance throughout the camp, and let every man kill his brother, every man his companion, and every man his neighbor.'" So the sons of Levi did according to the word of Moses. And about three thousand men of the people fell that day.*

Moses was able to help save the entire nation through intercession, but 3,000 perpetrators had to die to make that possible. These God-initiated deaths were not about cruelty and destruction but about protection and preservation. This is where the Levites earned their

Priesthood. The real question is, are we walking in the Priesthood to which we have been called?

In Numbers 13, God sent out twelve spies. Ten of them came back with an evil report concerning the land God was giving them. In Number 14:36,37 we are told,

> Now the men whom Moses sent to spy out the land, who returned and made all the congregation complain against him by bringing a bad report of the land, those very men who brought the evil report about the land, died by the plague before the Lord.

God killed all ten of the spies for bringing back an evil report to the congregation and it cost the nation another 40 years before they could go in and begin possessing the land.

Numbers 33:1-4 states,

> These are the journeys of the children of Israel, who went out of the land of Egypt by their armies under the hand of Moses and Aaron. Now Moses wrote down the starting points of their journeys at the command of the Lord. And these are their journeys according to their starting points: They departed from Rameses in the first month, on the fifteenth day of the first month; on the day after the Passover the children of Israel went out with **boldness** in the sight of all the Egyptians. For the Egyptians were burying all their firstborn, whom the Lord had killed among them. Also on their gods the Lord had executed judgments.

God paints a picture for the church concerning the issue of end-time boldness. Boldness in the Israelites was a product of watching the

Egyptian families bury their dead! If this principle holds, end-time boldness will be a product of the judgment of God. Isaiah 9:6,7 says,

> *For unto us a Child is born, Unto us a Son is given; And the government will be upon His shoulder. And His name will be called Wonderful, Counselor, Mighty God, Everlasting Father, Prince of Peace. Of the increase of His government and peace There will be no end, Upon the throne of David and over His kingdom, To order it and establish it with judgment and justice From that time forward, even forever. The zeal of the Lord of hosts will perform this.*

When we read this passage a question emerges – how will the zeal of God perform this? The zeal of God ignites and releases the boldness of His people! The zeal of God propelled Jesus to execute justice in the temple. Just like the zeal of God propelled Jesus to confront evil in the temple, the zeal of God in the last days will propel His own to judicially confront evil. Moses was required to confront evil. The judges were required to confront evil. The boldness that comes from God's demonstration of His judgment is what we can expect for the church in the last days. The Israelites rejoiced in boldness when they saw the Judicial Hand of God. *"Your people will be volunteers in the day of your power,"* Psalm 110 says. Are we practiced in boldly praying Spirit-inspired prayers? The day of God's power is accelerating! Zeal is coming!

Joshua 10 records an intervention that Israel did for the Gibeonites because of making covenant with them even though it was executed in deception! When surrounding cities heard that Gibeon had made peace with Israel, they decided to attack. Because the Gibeonites had executed a covenant with Israel, they sent messengers asking for help. So Joshua marched all night in order to attack the enemy.

Verse 11 tells us what we can expect when we go to war. But – only *if* there is no sin in the camp. It says, *"And it happened, as they fled before Israel and were on the descent of Beth Horon, that the Lord cast down large hailstones from heaven on them as far as Azekah, and they died. There were more who died from the hailstones than the children of Israel killed with the sword."* God intervened, and killed more than the Israelite armies. When going to war, we always want God on our side. That is why from the first formation of America's military, righteousness was encouraged and perversion was banned. Opening the military to homosexuality can be a death sentence for those who face battle! Sending our sons and daughters into combat with sin in the camp is abominable for many who once served!

In 1 Samuel 2:6, Hannah prophesies about the God who intervenes judicially. It says, *"The Lord kills and makes alive; He brings down to the grave and brings up."*

1 Samuel 6:19 tells us of God's intervention when the Israelites looked into the Ark of the Covenant. It says, *"Then He struck the men of Beth Shemesh, because they had looked into the ark of the Lord. He struck fifty thousand and seventy men of the people, and the people lamented because the Lord had struck the people with a great slaughter."* Love kills when rebellion threatens!

1 Chronicles 10:13 says, *"So Saul died for his unfaithfulness which he had committed against the Lord, because he did not keep the word of the Lord, and also because he consulted a medium for guidance."* We find that God killed Saul for unfaithfulness and because he did not inquire of the Lord. This passage is a good reminder that we exist in order to execute God's purpose and plan, not our own.

Psalm 55:15 records David's plea for covenant justice. It says, "*Let death seize them; Let them go down alive into hell, For wickedness is in their dwellings and among them.*" David prayed judgment on his friend for betrayal. Within a few months, his friend was in the grave. 2 Samuel 17:23 says, "*Now when Ahithophel saw that his advice was not followed, he saddled a donkey, and arose and went home to his house, to his city. Then he put his household in order, and hanged himself, and died; and he was buried in his father's tomb.*" Ahithophel was the wisest man in the Kingdom. He knew there was only a short window of opportunity to dethrone David and once it passed covenant justice would find the perpetrators.

Numbers 16:1-3 tells us about Korah, Dathan and Abiram and 250 leaders who came against Moses. Both Moses and David established enough trust in their relationship with God to expect His intervention when they were threatened. Since the Judge of all the Earth is no respecter of persons, when we develop that level of trust, we can expect the same result!

> *Now Korah the son of Izhar, the son of Kohath, the son of Levi, with Dathan and Abiram the sons of Eliab, and On the son of Peleth, sons of Reuben, took men; and they rose up before Moses with some of the children of Israel, two hundred and fifty leaders of the congregation, representatives of the congregation, men of renown. They gathered together against Moses and Aaron, and said to them, "You take too much upon yourselves, for all the congregation is holy, every one of them, and the Lord is among them. Why then do you exalt yourselves above the assembly of the Lord?"*

As near as we can tell, Moses declared verses 29-30,

If these men die naturally like all men, or if they are visited by the common fate of all men, then the Lord has not sent me. But if the Lord creates a new thing, and the earth opens its mouth and swallows them up with all that belongs to them, and they go down alive into the pit, then you will understand that these men have rejected the Lord.

God created a "sink hole" as a judgment. After Moses declared a new thing would happen to demonstrate that he had not done anything by his own will, we see his contribution in verse 15. Moses had to take a stand and pray judicially. He prayed accordingly and God tailor-made the judgment.

Verses 31-35 state,

Now it came to pass, as he finished speaking all these words, that the ground split apart under them, and the earth opened its mouth and swallowed them up, with their households and all the men with Korah, with all their goods. So they and all those with them went down alive into the pit; the earth closed over them, and they perished from among the assembly. Then all Israel who were around them fled at their cry, for they said, "Lest the earth swallow us up also!" And a fire came out from the Lord and consumed the two hundred and fifty men who were offering incense.

When Moses stopped praying, God intervened and put his critics in the grave. Can we grow to that place? In Isaiah 37, the entire nation of Israel was under assault, under Hezekiah's reign. The man who was coming against them was Sennacherib, King of Assyria. Hezekiah prayed against Sennacherib in Isaiah 37:16-20,

O Lord of hosts, God of Israel, the One who dwells between the cherubim, You are God, You alone, of all the kingdoms of the

earth. You have made heaven and earth. Incline Your ear, O Lord, and hear; open Your eyes, O Lord, and see; and hear all the words of Sennacherib, which he has sent to reproach the living God. Truly, Lord, the kings of Assyria have laid waste all the nations and their lands, and have cast their gods into the fire; for they were not gods, but the work of men's hands – wood and stone. Therefore they destroyed them. Now therefore, O Lord our God, save us from his hand, that all the kingdoms of the earth may know that You are the Lord, You alone.

This is covenantal, judicial prayer. Isaiah 37:21 says, *"Then Isaiah the son of Amoz sent to Hezekiah, saying, "Thus says the Lord God of Israel, 'Because you have prayed to Me **against** Sennacherib king of Assyria,..."* God heard Hezekiah's judicial prayer and answered. Priestly prayer is usually **for** while Kingly prayer is usually **against**!

The answer is described in verse 35-38,

"For I will defend this city, to save it For My own sake and for My servant David's sake." Then the angel of the Lord went out, and killed in the camp of the Assyrians one hundred and eighty-five thousand; and when people arose early in the morning, there were the corpses – all dead. So Sennacherib king of Assyria departed and went away, returned home, and remained at Nineveh. Now it came to pass, as he was worshiping in the house of Nisroch his god, that his sons Adrammelech and Sharezer struck him down with the sword; and they escaped into the land of Ararat. Then Esarhaddon his son reigned in his place.

God intervened for Israel and killed 185,000 in one night. The God of the Bible is a God whose love for His people intervenes when they are threatened. Kingly judicial prayer should be made against those who promote evil and advance perversion.

Jeremiah 20:1-6 describes the personal battle that Jeremiah found himself in with a false prophet. It says,

> *Now Pashhur the son of Immer, the priest who was also chief governor in the house of the Lord, heard that Jeremiah prophesied these things. Then Pashhur struck Jeremiah the prophet, and put him in the stocks that were in the high gate of Benjamin, which was by the house of the Lord. And it happened on the next day that Pashhur brought Jeremiah out of the stocks. Then Jeremiah said to him, "The Lord has not called your name Pashhur, but Magor-Missabib. For thus says the Lord: 'Behold, I will make you a terror to yourself and to all your friends; and they shall fall by the sword of their enemies, and your eyes shall see it. I will give all Judah into the hand of the king of Babylon, and he shall carry them captive to Babylon and slay them with the sword. Moreover I will deliver all the wealth of this city, all its produce, and all its precious things; all the treasures of the kings of Judah I will give into the hand of their enemies, who will plunder them, seize them, and carry them to Babylon. And you, Pashhur, and all who dwell in your house, shall go into captivity. You shall go to Babylon, and there you shall die, and be buried there, you and all your friends, to whom you have prophesied lies.'"*

The church of the last days is going to know the conflict of Jeremiah. That conflict is outlined in verses 7-13 of Jeremiah 20. It says,

O Lord, You induced me, and I was persuaded; You are stronger than I, and have prevailed. I am in derision daily; Everyone mocks me. For when I spoke, I cried out; I shouted, "Violence and plunder!" Because the word of the Lord was made to me A reproach and a derision daily. Then I said, "I will not make mention of Him, Nor speak anymore in His name." But His word was in my heart like a burning fire Shut up in my bones; I was weary of holding it back, And I could not. For I heard many mocking: "Fear on every side!" "Report," they say, "and we will report it!" All my acquaintances watched for my stumbling, saying, "Perhaps he can be induced; Then we will prevail against him, And we will take our revenge on him." But the Lord is with me as a mighty, awesome One. Therefore my persecutors will stumble, and will not prevail. They will be greatly ashamed, for they will not prosper. Their everlasting confusion will never be forgotten. But, O Lord of hosts, You who test the righteous, And see the mind and heart, Let me see Your vengeance on them; For I have pleaded my cause before You. Sing to the Lord! Praise the Lord! For He has delivered the life of the poor From the hand of evildoers.

Have the righteous pleaded their case before God against the wicked? If a politician promotes evil and the Spirit directs us, then our job is to plead judicially against him! All of us revere Jeremiah as a great prophet. But look at the pain and agony that carrying the prophetic word brought to him. He was hated and reproached. People looked for an opportunity to destroy him because they hated the plumbline of righteousness he brought. This is what it means to count the cost and be a Christian in the last days.

Jeremiah 28:1-10 outlines the conflict that Jeremiah had with a prophet named Hananiah. It says,

And it happened in the same year, at the beginning of the reign of Zedekiah king of Judah, in the fourth year and in the fifth month, that Hananiah the son of Azur the prophet, who was from Gibeon, spoke to me in the house of the Lord in the presence of the priests and of all the people, saying, "Thus speaks the Lord of hosts, the God of Israel, saying: 'I have broken the yoke of the king of Babylon. Within two full years I will bring back to this place all the vessels of the Lord's house, that Nebuchadnezzar king of Babylon took away from this place and carried to Babylon. And I will bring back to this place Jeconiah the son of Jehoiakim, king of Judah, with all the captives of Judah who went to Babylon,' says the Lord, 'for I will break the yoke of the king of Babylon.'" Then the prophet Jeremiah spoke to the prophet Hananiah in the presence of the priests and in the presence of all the people who stood in the house of the Lord, and the prophet Jeremiah said, "Amen! The Lord do so; the Lord perform your words which you have prophesied, to bring back the vessels of the Lord's house and all who were carried away captive, from Babylon to this place. Nevertheless hear now this word that I speak in your hearing and in the hearing of all the people: The prophets who have been before me and before you of old prophesied against many countries and great kingdoms – of war and disaster and pestilence. As for the prophet who prophesies of peace, when the word of the prophet comes to pass, the prophet will be known as one whom the Lord has truly sent." Then Hananiah the prophet took the yoke off the prophet Jeremiah's neck and broke it.

God had just given Jeremiah an opposite word. He revealed that if the country wanted to prosper, they needed to submit. In verses 11-17 we are told,

And Hananiah spoke in the presence of all the people, saying, "Thus says the Lord: 'Even so I will break the yoke of Nebuchadnezzar king of Babylon from the neck of all nations within the space of two full years.'" And the prophet Jeremiah went his way. Now the word of the Lord came to Jeremiah, after Hananiah the prophet had broken the yoke from the neck of the prophet Jeremiah, saying, "Go and tell Hananiah, saying, 'Thus says the Lord: "You have broken the yokes of wood, but you have made in their place yokes of iron." For thus says the Lord of hosts, the God of Israel: "I have put a yoke of iron on the neck of all these nations, that they may serve Nebuchadnezzar king of Babylon; and they shall serve him. I have given him the beasts of the field also."'" Then the prophet Jeremiah said to Hananiah the prophet, "Hear now, Hananiah, the Lord has not sent you, but you make this people trust in a lie. Therefore thus says the Lord: 'Behold, I will cast you from the face of the earth. This year you shall die, because you have taught rebellion against the Lord.'" So Hananiah the prophet died the same year in the seventh month.

Three months after Jeremiah declared the judgment of God on Hananiah, Hananiah died. God intervened to prove who was His and who the counterfeit was. Many times we discount something because it is Old Testament or Old Covenant. But Acts 5:1-11 is *not* Old Testament and it confirms that God does intervene with judgment. This judgment is the resurrected Christ killing Ananias and Sapphira because they were about to sow the spirit of mammon into the congregation. Verse 32 states that all had been delivered from this spirit, when nobody said that anything he possessed was his own. God cemented the deliverance from the spirit of mammon by judging Ananias and Sapphira. By cutting Ananias and Sapphira off, He ensured all the future churches who would be started, as a result of the persecution of Stephen would have the fear of the Lord in their foundation. Jesus has not changed. He is the same yesterday, today and forever. The fear of the Lord has to be restored! He sets a boundary for wickedness and intervenes judicially. The same God who put 185,000 in the grave to save Jerusalem is still willing to visit today. The same God who intervened to save Peter's life by killing Herod in Acts 12, has not changed! He *is* the same today! The same Jesus who killed all the firstborn of Egypt, says in Revelation 6:8 He will intervene and one fourth of the earth's population will be destroyed. In Revelation 9:18, the same Jesus who brought the flood says that one third of the earth will be destroyed. The same God who, in Revelation 17:7-9, cuts off His people for demon worship, pronounced judgment in Romans 1:23, on what He called nature-worship. Romans 1:23 says, "*...and changed the glory of the incorruptible God into an image made like corruptible man – and birds and four-footed animals and creeping things.*" The same Jesus who destroyed Sodom and Gomorrah says in Romans 1:32 that those who promote and practice sexual sin will face the Judge who destroys. God judges because He is Love. His love sets a boundary for the wicked so they cannot destroy a harvest field. Let the Jesus who intervenes judicially rise on behalf of the church in these last days. Let us be committed to demonstrating the fullness of His love!

♦ Al Houghton ♦

Chapter 14

Love Executes Justice

Revelation 22:10-13 states, *"And he said to me, 'Do not seal the words of the prophecy of this book, for the time is at hand. He who is unjust, let him be unjust still; he who is filthy, let him be filthy still; he who is righteous, let him be righteous still; he who is holy, let him be holy still. And behold, I am coming quickly, and My reward is with Me, to give to every one according to his work. I am the Alpha and the Omega, the Beginning and the End, the First and the Last.'"*

This passage pictures the conflict between God and satan, good and evil, the church and the world! The Word 'still' is applied to those representing both good and evil groups! Richard Henry Weymouth's translation of this passage has a footnote explaining the Greek word translated *"still."* Weymouth indicates **et-ee**/*"still"* refers to the crystallization and development of character until each side fully represents the 'gods' or God they serve. The unjust grow more brazen in stealing, killing and destroying until they look like satan himself. The righteous grow into the likeness of Jesus, which means they also execute divine judgment on the unjust and filthy representing the Jesus of Revelation. The reward of verse 12 is the anointing to remove the defiling elements from the harvest field by praying justice on the unjust and judgment on the filthy before they destroy the nation. Jesus as the Alpha and Omega, the beginning and the end, promises to save our harvest field – and He will use covenant love to do it. The church's purpose in Ephesians 3 is to make principalities and powers know that they *do not* rule. The filthy grow more and more perverse, but the holy grow more and more holy.

The foundation for all five layers of God's love in the New Testament is outlined in Ephesians. Paul prays that we discover the fullness of God's love! Ephesians 3:14-20 states,

> *For this reason I bow my knees to the Father of our Lord Jesus Christ, from whom the whole family in heaven and earth is named, that He would grant you, according to the riches of His glory, to be strengthened with might through His Spirit in the inner man, that Christ may dwell in your hearts through faith; that you, being rooted and grounded in love, may be able to comprehend with all the saints what is the width and length and depth and height – to know the love of Christ which passes knowledge; that you may be filled with all the fullness of God. Now to Him who is able to do exceedingly abundantly above all that we ask or think, according to the power that works in us,...*

The first thing we want to note regarding Paul's prayer of intercession is that he understood every believer was to be rooted and grounded, or *matured*, in the love of God. I would like to suggest the maturing process has five identifiable dimensions which, in total, comprise the fullness of Christ. Paul even makes it clear that only when we are matured in the love of God can we demonstrate God's fullness! The language of Ephesians 3:17-19 seems to equate the five layers of love with the fullness of Christ!

I believe that verse 19, in effect, defines the "fullness of God" as five layers of love. When we identity all five layers and prepare to demonstrate them, what Paul prayed becomes a reality. Demonstrating the fullness of Christ brings biblical victories. Ephesians continues to elaborate on that definition in the very next chapter as God introduces five offices assigned as agents to bring love to maturity.

We are told in Ephesians 4:11-13, *"And He Himself gave some to be apostles, some prophets, some evangelists, and some pastors and teachers, for the equipping of the saints for the work of ministry, for the edifying of the body of Christ, till we all come to the unity of the faith and of the knowledge of the Son of God, to a* **tel-i-os**/*perfect man, to the measure of the stature of the fullness of Christ;..."* Jesus commands us to love like God loves in Matthew 5:48. Our question and our prayers should always be, which layer is appropriate for what we face? Isn't it interesting that Paul defines the fullness of God as our understanding of and willingness to move in the five layers of God's love? In the very next chapter he assigns the **tel-i-os/**maturing of the church to the five ministry gifts. Paul identifies apostles, prophets, evangelists, pastors and teachers as agents on a mission. He then tells us their function is to grow the church into the **tel-i-os**/maturity of the fullness of Christ. When the fullness of Christ is present, demonized resistance is dealt with.

Paul connects the five-fold ministry with the assignment to grow the church in each layer of God's love. In Verses 14-16 it says, *"...that we should no longer be children, tossed to and fro and carried about with every wind of doctrine, by the trickery of men, in the cunning craftiness of deceitful plotting, but, speaking the truth in love, may grow up in all things into Him who is the head – Christ – from whom the whole body, joined and knit together by what every joint supplies, according to the effective working by which every part does its share, causes growth of the body for the edifying of itself in love."* The church will grow to maturity when all five inputs are freely embraced and allowed to flow in our Christian training. 1 Corinthians 12 makes it clear that there is tremendous difference in the variety and operation of ministries. Not every ministry is "turn-the-other-cheek"-centered, but every ministry contributes in some way to God's covenantal care and love of His people.

Several decades ago, the Lord gave me a vision of the ascension. I saw Jesus rise in the clouds, enter into heaven and take a seat at the right Hand of God. What happened next was the real surprise. He reached into His chest, pulled out His Heart and threw it toward the earth. When His Heart hit the ionosphere, it splintered into five pieces. Each one of those five pieces went down to the church and merged with the hearts of various individuals. Then the vision changed to all five pieces, one at a time, cycling through the pulpit. When the last piece of the merged Heart of God cycled through the pulpit, then the congregation stood up en mass and they *looked exactly like Jesus*. There was no difference.

The end-time army of the Lord is forming. Isaiah 11:1-4 describes them,

> *There shall come forth a Rod from the stem of Jesse, And a Branch shall grow out of his roots. The Spirit of the Lord shall rest upon Him, The Spirit of wisdom and understanding, The Spirit of counsel and might, The Spirit of knowledge and of the fear of the Lord. His delight is in the fear of the Lord, And He shall not judge by the sight of His eyes, Nor decide by the hearing of His ears; But with righteousness He shall judge the poor, And decide with equity for the meek of the earth; He shall strike the earth with the rod of His mouth, And with the breath of His lips He shall slay the wicked.*

Embracing the message of this book empowers the church to walk in this realm of the Spirit!

◆ God's Layered Love ◆

◆ Al Houghton ◆

Chapter 15

The Love that Saves, Also Cuts Off

Acts 13 contains Paul's longest recorded message in the New Testament. The subject and length of the inclusion testifies to the importance of this core message to the formation of the early church. Paul preached the covenant of Sure Mercy that God gave David and that Jesus guaranteed to the church with His resurrection. Acts 13:21-23 says,

> *And afterward they asked for a king; so God gave them Saul the son of Kish, a man of the tribe of Benjamin, for forty years. And when He had removed him, He raised up for them David as king, to whom also He gave testimony and said, "I have found David the son of Jesse, a man after My own heart, who will do all My will.' From this man's seed, according to the promise, God raised up for Israel a Savior – Jesus – ...*

Jesus came as a representative of the house of David. He ascended to fulfill the prophetic promises God gave David!

Verses 32-34 state, *"And we declare to you glad tidings – that promise which was made to the fathers. God has fulfilled this for us their children, in that He has raised up Jesus. As it is also written in the second Psalm: 'You are My Son, Today I have begotten You.' And that He raised Him from the dead, no more to return to corruption, He has spoken thus:*

'I will give you the sure mercies of David.'" The Davidic covenant guarantees a unique depth of God's love. Now if we want to know what Jesus guarantees us from David's covenant, we have to go back to the place where it was first given to David in 2 Samuel 7! When I was ministering for the first time in Germany, the Lord asked me, "When did I speak to my servant David about his son Solomon, before or after he met Bathsheba?"

We all know that the apex of David's failure in sin was killing Uriah the Hittite and taking Uriah's wife Bathsheba. We also know that Solomon came out of David and Bathsheba's union. But when the Lord asked me about the timeline of David's sin versus God's covenant, I had to investigate. I found the Lord gave David a covenant of Sure Mercy at the same time He spoke to David about Solomon. And this occurred in 2 Samuel 7, exactly four Bible chapters before David met Bathsheba.

God gave David a covenant of Sure Mercy and spoke to him about Solomon **before** David fell into sin with Bathsheba. Sure Mercy is God's promise to redeem our failures even before we ever commit them. God redeemed David's failure four chapters before he committed adultery! Verse 15 says, *"But My mercy shall not depart from him, as I took it from Saul, whom I removed from before you."* If we review Saul's loss of his kingdom, we discover he lost it because he would not execute biblical justice. The loss of his kingdom had three elements. First, he lost his **office** of king. Second, he lost his **call** to be king over Israel. Third, he lost the **anointing** to walk in the office and fulfill the call. We know there is a distinction between office and call because David was temporarily displaced from his office by Absalom, but because David's call was not removed and because he practiced true repentance, his office was restored. The covenant of Sure Mercy guaranteed David's restoration and his enemy's destruction. David prayed his covenant in Psalm 143:12 and Absalom was executed.

Invoking the covenant of Sure Mercy brings the Sword of the Lord against those who want to possess our harvest field for their own purposes. It has its judicial origin in the Abrahamic Covenant where God said, *"Those who bless you, I will bless and those who curse you, I will curse."* God was serious with Abraham and biblical justice advanced by covenant! The covenant of Sure Mercy is a two-edged sword. Edge One cuts away personal failure. Edge Two cuts off an enemy who refuses to relent, like Absalom.

The covenant of Sure Mercy has three primary elements. "Sure Mercy" means that if we have a failure, we do not have to lose our **office**, we do not have to lose our **call** and we do not have to lose the **anointing** of the Spirit to walk in the office and fulfill the call. Paul is warning in Acts 13 not to take lightly the covenant of Sure Mercy because if we do, we can lose our city or nation. This is exactly what happened to Israel. They lost Jerusalem to utter destruction in 70 AD and they lost their nation. So the same God who saves also cuts Israel off for disobedience and rebellion.

Now we live in the most exciting time in history. We live in the days when God has restored the Jewish nation and those who will hear are going to accept their Messiah. The same Jesus who saves also cuts off as a manifestation of love. If God was not willing to cut off those attempting to destroy the Jewish harvest, then He would not satisfy covenant love. In covenant love, God promises to cut off the enemy who will not cease trying to destroy our destiny or our harvest. In order for covenant love to save it must *also* cut off. This was Paul's message. In 2 Peter chapters 1 and 2 it was Peter's message. God's love both saves *and* judges.

In 2 Peter 1, he talks about experiencing God and being saved. He says in verses 15-21,

> *For we did not follow cunningly devised fables when we made known to you the power and coming of our Lord Jesus Christ, but were eyewitnesses of His majesty. For He received from God the Father honor and glory when such a voice came to Him from the Excellent Glory: "This is My beloved Son, in whom I am well pleased." And we heard this voice which came from heaven when we were with Him on the holy mountain. And so we have the prophetic word confirmed, which you do well to heed as a light that shines in a dark place, until the day dawns and the morning star rises in your hearts; knowing this first, that no prophecy of Scripture is of any private interpretation, for prophecy never came by the will of man, but holy men of God spoke as they were moved by the Holy Spirit.*

Peter made it clear that everyone who believed on the sure words of Scripture would be eternally rewarded. Jesus is alive! There is no other name given, whereby we must be saved! When Jesus ascended, He became Judge of all the Earth!

In Chapter 2, Peter also made it clear that there would be false prophets and false teachers that would bring in destructive and damning heresies. He explained that there will be covetous counterfeits who would pervert Scripture for their own gain. Claiming that there is no judgment today may qualify! Peter went on to say that the very same love that saves will utterly destroy every one of the heretics. Peter was not seeker-sensitive. He said some people are like dogs that return to their vomit and like pigs that return to wallowing in their mire. People who walk that pattern meet the Judge! And the same love that saves *will* cut them off. There is one thing we need to understand about God's love: it is a two-edged sword. It will save us eternally *and* it will cut away our sin. For those who deliberately, defiantly and consistently choose to dishonor God's Word, it will cut them off and can put them in the grave forever. Make no mistake about it: there is nothing like the love of God and nothing like the Sword of the Spirit when it comes to dealing with the rebellious and the disobedient.

I believe God's love has five different layers. The fullness of Christ is represented by five-fold ministry. It saves and ultimately, it will cut off, depending on which application is needed at the time. Every situation is different and we must seek the Spirit to lead us to the appropriate course of action by prayer. The fullness of Christ awaits every believer who says, "I choose to mature to the place where I love as God loves!" Search the Scripture for everyone God resurrected and count them. Search the Scripture for everyone God terminated or threatened to and number them. Which anointing do we hold in highest esteem? Which anointing dominates Revelation? Which one is greater? Then remember love is the source of *both* actions. It is only in loving the way God loves that we can reach the fullness of Christ. For those who may face the opposition of an Elymas or the destruction of a Herod, growing in mature-love may determine whether we finish our heavenly assignment or go home early! It is my great hope that this truth gets established in every believer and we all finish our race victoriously!

Chapter 16

Love Never Fails

1 Corinthians 13 is a very familiar chapter to most believers. We call it the 'Love Chapter.' Almost every message we have heard on this chapter has probably been given from a Priestly perspective. But since Peter's proclamation in Acts 2:36, we are forced to view this chapter equally from a Kingly perspective. Peter said in Acts 2:36, *"Therefore let all the house of Israel know assuredly that God has made this Jesus, whom you crucified, both Lord and Christ."* Is there a Kingly side to *"love never fails"*?

1 Corinthians 13:1-8 says,

Though I speak with the tongues of men and of angels, but have not love, I have become sounding brass or a clanging cymbal. And though I have the gift of prophecy, and understand all mysteries and all knowledge, and though I have all faith, so that I could remove mountains, but have not love, I am nothing. And though I bestow all my goods to feed the poor, and though I give my body to be burned, but have not love, it profits me nothing. Love suffers long and is kind; love does not envy; love does not parade itself, is not puffed up; does not behave rudely, does not seek its own, is not provoked, thinks no evil; does not rejoice in iniquity, but rejoices in the truth; bears all things, believes all *things, hopes all things, endures all things. **Love never fails**. But whether there are prophecies, they will fail; whether there are tongues, they will cease; whether there is knowledge, it will vanish away.*

"*Love never fails*" is one of the strongest promises that we have in Scripture. We are told that prophecies will fail, tongues will cease and knowledge will vanish away. But love never fails. This is perhaps the greatest covenantal promise and it should be set in both the Priestly and Kingly realms. By emphasizing Priestly love for the last fifty years, the church has become a lopsided lover. We love enemies that God would remove. Even though the Kingly side of love has definite applications, the Priestly has been emphasized making it passive in the face of evil. If love never fails then love conquers evil. But when does love terminate an enemy so that we can finish our race? James was martyred by Herod. The early church would have thought James was the favored one and Peter the slighted one. The more I read the early church fathers, the more I became amazed at their embrace and expectation of martyrdom. They felt cheated if it passed them by! Hebrews 11:35 describes those who were tortured not accepting deliverance that they might obtain a better resurrection. It is obvious that many really believed in the better resurrection! Hebrews 11:35 says, "*Women received their dead raised to life again. Others were tortured, not accepting deliverance, that they might obtain a better resurrection.*" This passage indicates there is a better resurrection based on what we endure! (See *Marked Men* for the early church's expectation of a better resurrection and for a glimpse of their expectations in their own words.)

While God's love allowed James to be martyred, it killed Herod so Peter could finish his race. Love never fails because all those who are sacrificed gain a better resurrection! Radical Islam is bent on martyring

Christians and we see many such events in Africa, Asia, the Middle East and other nations. Is love failing believers, or are they fulfilling the biblical prophecy we see in Revelation? Does love **always** mean that Christians will be martyred in a conflict with the enemy? Or does love promise a divine intervention, if we *yet* have an assignment to fulfill? James was martyred while Peter got the intervention. The promise that *"Love never fails"* is a two-edged sword! One edge allowed Herod to martyr James. The other edge weighed to Herod in justice what Herod weighed to James. Faith for judicial love should grow into manifestations! Judicial prayer asks God to weigh to politicians and people groups according to their works. When Jesus visits in Revelation, He rewards **according to their works**. All those who champion abortion, may one day find themselves aborted!

1 Corinthians 13:9-13 states, *"For we know in part and we prophesy in part. But when that which is perfect has come, then that which is in part will be done away. When I was a child, I spoke as a child, I understood as a child, I thought as a child; but when I became a man, I put away childish things. For now we see in a mirror, dimly, but then face to face. Now I know in part, but then I shall know just as I also am known. And now abide faith, hope, love, these three; but the greatest of these is love."* The exhortation in 1 Corinthians 13 is that we grow up! We are exhorted to not simply view love as one-sided. The love of God does not overlook and forgive everything, as the majority of the church believes. The love of God is not carte-blanche forgiveness for anything and everything. A childish view of the love of God is, "I can do anything I want to and God will forgive me." That is presumptuous sin and guaranteed judgment. Does the love of God judge evil and remove those who perpetrate it? The clear answer to that, in the book of Revelation, is yes! Can we mature in the love of God and accurately discern the Priestly approach from the Kingly approach? Can we mature in both and allow both to keep their roots in the Holy Spirit's application

of the love of God? I believe we can, just as the early church did. Herod was the consummate example of *"Love never fails"*! Peter was thankful for the remainder of his life! Covenantal love terminated Herod and that love still terminates today!

John 3:16-18 states, *"For God so loved the world that He gave His only begotten Son, that whoever believes in Him should not perish but have everlasting life. For God did not send His Son into the world to condemn the world, but that the world through Him might be saved. He who believes in Him is not condemned; but he who does not believe is condemned already, because he has not believed in the name of the only begotten Son of God."* This is the Jesus we are all familiar with. Except, the love of God in John 3:16 has some qualifiers that become evident immediately in verses 17,18. Verse 17 says the Father did not send the Son to judge the world. But the very next verse says that he who believes is not judged, but he who does not believe **is judged *already***. The very act of rejecting the saving, sacrificing Christ brings us into judgment, according to verse 18. How can Bible-reading believers deny there is any judgment at all? Verse 18 makes it clear that there *is* judgment and it comes to those who say no to the Savior. When people reject the love of God, demonstrated by Jesus, they step over into a place of judgment. Love saves, but the rejection of love judges. About this, the New Testament is extremely clear!

The next two verses of John 3 expand on that judgment! It says, *"And this is the condemnation, that the light has come into the world, and men loved darkness rather than light, because their deeds were evil. For everyone practicing evil hates the light and does not come to the light, lest his deeds should be exposed."* There is a solid reason why people say no and reject the love of God. It is because they love their sin. Some people choose evil over God's love. How does love never fail in that situation? If people reject the love of God, then the judgment of

God comes on them! The love of God is, in fact, a two-edged sword. It never fails to save. But for those who reject it, it never fails to judge. Love never fails! Love carried James to the completion of his ministry and simultaneously filled the cup for Herod's removal!

1 John 4:7,8 says, *"Beloved, let us love one another, for love is of God; and everyone who loves is born of God and knows God. He who does not love does not know God, for God is love."* We know that God is love. The fact that God is love means that **everything** He does has its roots and its motivation in love. Sacrificing His life to save us has its roots and motivation in love. Judging those who want to destroy us has its roots and motivation in love. Any parent knows love for their children includes protecting against predators. I learned early on the farm that *if we expected to eat*, when predators came after our animals – we had to kill the predators! If we did not kill the foxes, we did not have eggs – because our chickens were fox-food! When the foxes came to destroy the hens, we did not welcome them with open arms but blew them to smithereens! When wolves came for our cattle, we had to kill the wolves. David, the great shepherd, killed the predators. The lion and the bear died at David's hand. Have any predators died at your hand? Are there wolves after our children and grandchildren? Are there wolves after our cities? Are there wolves after our nation? How does the love of God respond to wolves? Does love kill in order to save? Would you kill a mountain lion if it threatened your children? Would you kill a bear if it threatened them? If God *is* love, and if we are to *love the way God loves*, then there is both an application of love that saves and an application of love that kills in order to save. Why have we only grown in Priestly love, when it is obvious that the Bible is balanced with both the Priestly and the Kingly? Prayer that moves God's Hand against predators is a biblical thing to do! Not doing it is dangerous, even criminal neglect. Hirelings abandon their flock to the wolves. True shepherds do not! Isn't it time we all did some shepherding? Praying

political wolves into their eternal reward under the unction of the Holy Spirit is a biblical responsibility that has eternal reward!

Love is perfected when our prayers move God's Hands in both dimensions of the Kingly and Priestly as the Holy Spirit directs. When the Holy Spirit directs a Priestly response, then we offer salvation. But when the Holy Spirit directs a judicial response, then we initiate judgment by praying it in the Throne-Room. Love is perfected when we can move with Jesus and love as He loved! God loved Peter enough to remove Herod! Does God love us enough to remove our predators? Identify the political predators in your nation. They shed innocent blood and support what God hates. The enemies of your nation will be God-haters by their actions. God-haters champion antichrist, antibible positions. Hate-speech laws, abortion and gay marriage are examples. Psalm 68:1,2 in the New Living Translation is exactly what David prayed over his opposition, *"Rise up, O God, and scatter your enemies. Let those who hate God run for their lives. Blow them away like smoke. Melt them like wax in a fire. Let the wicked perish in the presence of God."* We have David's covenant and should pray like he prayed! Pray like David prayed! We want God's Presence that heals just like the early church. The same Presence that healed them all, killed Ananias and Sapphira in fulfilling Psalm 68:1,*"Let God arise, Let His enemies be scattered. Let those also who hate Him flee before Him."* In Revelation 2, Jesus fights against the wicked with the Sword of His Mouth!

In Hebrews 1:1-3 we are told, *"God, who at various times and in various ways spoke in time past to the fathers by the prophets, has in these last days spoken to us by His Son, whom He has appointed heir of all things, through whom also He made the worlds; who being the brightness of His glory and the express image of His person, and upholding all things by the word of His power, when He had by Himself purged our sins, sat down at the right hand of the Majesty on high,..."*

Since Jesus is the Express Image of the Person of the Father, then we know that when we love like Jesus loved, we have the perfect example of how the love of God functions, operates and acts. That means when we watch Jesus in action, we have all the different manifestations of the love of God. Did Jesus clean house in the temple? Did He kill a fig tree? Did He say that we would do the same thing? Yes, yes and yes! Jesus laid His life down in love. But He also expressed a judicial side of love. *"Love never fails..."* when we make the right application in agreement with the Holy Spirit. If there is a wolf and we enable that wolf by praying **for** him instead of **against** him, it shows we have a foolish and immature understanding of the love of God. Could it be we are working against God's plans by enabling evil instead of arresting it? According to Jesus, tradition makes the Word of none effect. If we refuse to step into the Kingly judicial side of the love that never fails, we facilitate the rule of evil! If we love our spouses and kids enough to protect them from predators, we must understand that God loves our nation enough to protect it from predators. When we pray judicial prayers, it institutes our judicial covenant. Is there not enough love of God to honor and guarantee the purpose of the founders of our nation? As directed by the Spirit, we must be willing to pray **against** the wolves instead of **for** them. If we do not understand that praying against evil by the direction of the Holy Spirit is the love of God in action, then we are blinded by a religious spirit. Instead of packaging the Loving Christ for mass-marketing, let us seek to know who He truly is, in His fullness. Projecting God's love means leading people to Christ as both Savior and Judge. Praying wolves into judgment is just as eternally rewarding as praying individuals into heaven. If the church had prayed Hitler into judgment, millions of lives would have been saved! Through historical fact, we know more Christians were killed by Hitler than Jews! *"Love never fails"* means you can pray wolves into termination, sparing many innocent sheep!

Hebrews 8:1-6 says, *"Now this is the main point of the things we are saying: We have such a High Priest, who is seated at the right hand of the throne of the Majesty in the heavens, a Minister of the sanctuary and of the true tabernacle which the Lord erected, and not man. For every high priest is appointed to offer both gifts and sacrifices. Therefore it is necessary that this One also have something to offer. For if He were on earth, He would not be a priest, since there are priests who offer the gifts according to the law; who serve the copy and shadow of the heavenly things, as Moses was divinely instructed when he was about to make the tabernacle. For He said, 'See that you make all things according to the pattern shown you on the mountain.' But now He has obtained a more excellent ministry, inasmuch as He is also Mediator of a **better covenant, which was established on better promises**."* We have a New Covenant, based on better promises. Many leaders declare God is grace. Jesus took all judgment for us and therefore, 'God is love' means we do not have to face judgment anymore. So the real question is a simple one – does love cut off in order to save? Does the love of God terminate in order to save? There are many believers carrying a message of 'Ultimate Grace.' This message either leaves the impression, or says outright, that Jesus died for all judgment and **there is no more judgment**. But nothing could be further from the truth! This is an open refusal to accept the reality of the love of God in both the Priestly and Kingly realms. This effectively takes a scalpel to Scripture. I do not know about you, but the last time I tried to ignore or remove something from the Word, the result was not spiritual growth, but a spiritual arrest.

We do have a better covenant and it is based on better promises. But it is obvious in the book of Revelation that love terminates in order to save. Denying that or trying to redefine it should be characterized for what it is – apostasy! The fruit of an 'Ultimate Grace' message leads to unbridled people doing whatever they want because they have no standard of righteousness. Righteousness is completely obviated by redefining Jesus as One who blesses and never judges. That Jesus is an invention of a sinner's mind who prefers not to face the Judicial Christ. Denial does not work with God! Every person must stand before the Judgment Seat of Christ! Will we see many believers sent away or losing their reward for feeding and befriending wolves? I suspect we will!

Hebrews 13:8,9 says, *"Jesus Christ is the same yesterday, today, and forever. Do not be carried about with various and strange doctrines. For it is good that the heart be established by grace, not with foods which have not profited those who have been occupied with them."* Jesus is declared to be the same in the New Testament as He was in the Old. He is the same yesterday, today and forever. I suspect He is concerned at how He is portrayed today. We were warned about these days in Hebrews 13:9, and what we are hearing today qualifies as a *"...strange doctrine."* I do not think it is a surprise that He mentions *"grace"* right after the *"strange doctrine."* Jesus is the love that never fails and His actions, by the Holy Spirit, demonstrate who He is as both Priest and King. The fact that Jesus killed Ananias and Sapphira is a real thorn in the flesh for Ultimate Grace-ers! It proves their bogus assumption erroneous. I thank God for grace and want all God has for every single one of us – but if I lead believers to **presume** on it, then I am guilty of manslaughter! If a leader teaches presumptuous, unbiblical grace, he or she must answer for the condition of the flock. Ultimate Grace can only thrive where there is no fear of the Lord! Hebrews 10:26,29 says, *"For if we sin willfully after we have received the knowledge of the truth, there no longer remains a sacrifice for sins,...Of how much worse punishment, do you suppose, will he be thought worthy who has trampled the Son of God underfoot, counted the blood of the covenant by which he was sanctified a common thing, and insulted the Spirit of grace?"* The message of Ultimate Grace is an insult to the "Spirit of grace"! We cannot pick and choose our favorite passages to cling to. Cutting and pasting Scripture or taking a sharp pair of scissors to our Bible will impact our maturity and limit our understanding of Christ and our relationship with God. If a passage makes us uncomfortable we must study and not just reject it!

Ultimate grace is refuted in Acts 4 and 5 where the early church agrees together, crying out for a display of the Judicial Christ! If having a New Covenant that is based on better promises means only grace, then someone needs to rewrite Acts 5:1-5. They, in fact, should rewrite history altogether. In Acts 5:1-5, bearers of destruction tried to reintroduce the spirit of mammon into a congregation that had been cleansed. Love never fails. And God's love for the church, in Acts 5:1-5, meant judgment on evil. Peter made reference to the issue of lying to the Holy Spirit over the issue of money. Love killed Ananias and Sapphira. Are there wolves, spiritual, political or otherwise, that will not relent? Are there wolves that need a withering-roots declaration? Love never fails. Does God love the potential harvest of nations enough to deal with the wolves? Are we willing to ask Him? God does care deeply and I believe is soon to move dramatically in the church, calling leaders back to their First Love!

Why would love terminate Ananias and Sapphira? That is an excellent question. Perhaps we can find an answer in Luke 16:1-8. It is obvious that the steward in this passage parallels Ananias in his attitude. When the steward was called into account and realized he was about to be fired, he immediately set into motion a manipulation in order to gain an advantage. He used his position to reduce what people owed by as much as half. In order to be received, and to further his self-interest, he compromised the standard. Is there anywhere else we can think of where men and women are tempted to compromise the standard in order to be received? Do we see men and women compromising standards to build a larger or bigger church? An important Scriptural question for us is, how much truth do we owe to the flock? As ministers, do we owe people what they want and expect to hear? Or do we owe them what God says? Is there a temptation to only present partial-truths, in order to be better received? This modern-day phenomenon has built some of the larger ministries in America. We see a watering-down of Scripture's standards of courage, morality and purity. By being silent on a subject, we give tacit approval. Thyatira tried that centuries ago and got rebuked for it! Luke 16:8 is very interesting, in that light. The manipulative steward is commended because his manipulation worked. The real question is, what is the price of the manipulation? Everlasting habitation means **hell**! Does love remove in order to save? It did in dealing with Ananias and Sapphira. Will love remove compromising shepherds, prophets, teachers, evangelists and apostles? Under the Holy Spirit's unction, we know it will!

Matthew 10:27,28 says, *"Whatever I tell you in the dark, speak in the light; and what you hear in the ear, preach on the housetops. And do not fear those who kill the body but cannot kill the soul. But rather fear Him who is able to destroy both soul and body in hell."* Jesus was very clear about the standard for ministry. We cannot diminish the Word. If we diminish the Word, we are in danger of judgment. He said, *"Do not fear those who kill the body but cannot kill the soul. But rather fear Him who is able to destroy both soul and body in hell."* Jesus told the Twelve that the One they had to fear was the God who, after He kills the body, can destroy the soul in hell, forever. Is this the same Jesus we hear preached today? Jesus confirmed the fact that when God kills, He kills twice. The first time it is just the body. But the next part is much more serious. Does love kill in order to save? It would appear that it does. The Holy Spirit's removal of Ananias and Sapphira is historical fact and an undeniable, biblical reality. I suspect that church history is also full of more terminations than these. Does love kill in order to save? It certainly does and Jesus made it quite clear. We need to know God and His righteous standard. It is perilous not to. Why should wolves be allowed to ravage innocent people? By praying **for** evil leaders, we enable their destructive ways to continue and effectively become **complicit** in their evil deeds! The Judgment Seat of Christ will hold no joy for those believers!

Luke 16:10-13 says, *"He who is faithful in what is least is faithful also in much; and he who is unjust in what is least is unjust also in much. Therefore if you have not been faithful in the unrighteous mammon, who will commit to your trust the true riches? And if you have not been faithful in what is another man's, who will give you what is your own? No servant can serve two masters; for either he will hate the one and love the other, or else he will be loyal to the one and despise the other. You cannot serve God and mammon."* Jesus made it clear that we cannot serve two masters. We cannot serve both God and money, because the two require opposite responses from God's love. When we worship God, love blesses. When we worship mammon, love kills! The New Testament church was completely cleansed from the spirit of mammon. But Ananias tried to bring it back into the Body. In this case, love for the New Testament church intervened and judged the spirit of mammon, and saved the Body from defilement. It is obvious that love terminates in order to save. Now the question becomes, **when** do we pray for love to terminate in order to save? If this standard returns to pulpits, who will be left standing? This standard started the church-age and this standard will finish it!

Jesus made it clear that the religious system of the Pharisees was totally defiled. That is likely why He cleaned house in the temple twice. He did it in the beginning of His ministry and again at the end of His ministry. But He did go on to say that we would do the same thing –

speak to a mountain and it would be removed. That was after He killed the fig tree as an example. So the real question for us is, when do we pray that the love of God will manifest by terminating in order to save? What is the standard that brings the love of God that terminates? When does a nation need to be saved from its own elected officials? When do sheep need to be saved from their own chosen ministries? What overriding issue pushes us into requesting that God terminate? Why in Acts 5, did love terminate Ananias and Sapphira? Was it solely for lying to the Holy Spirit or was there a different reason? The second filling of the Holy Spirit in Acts 4:31 had immediate fruit! Acts 5:31,32 says, "...*Him God has exalted to His right hand to be Prince and Savior, to give repentance to Israel and forgiveness of sins. And we are His witnesses to these things, and so also is the Holy Spirit whom God has given to those who obey Him.*" No one said anything he had was his own.

Acts 4:34-37 describes the new standard of commitment,

Nor was there anyone among them who lacked; for all who were possessors of lands or houses sold them, and brought the proceeds of the things that were sold, and laid them at the apostles' feet; and they distributed to each as anyone had need. And Joses, who was also named Barnabas by the apostles (which is translated Son of Encouragement), a Levite of the country of Cyprus, having land, sold it, and brought the money and laid it at the apostles' feet.

Why did Ananias and Sapphira lie? To make it appear as if they also embraced the standard when they had not? This meant love-of-money was an open door and perilous inroad for evil into the foundation of the early church. Money-manipulation was a violation of being delivered from "...*Neither did anyone say anything he possessed was his own...*"

and consequently was a terminating offense! The Holy Spirit initiates the appropriate prayers if we have the governmental understanding of God's covenant!

The real question we come to at this stage is, does God hate evil so much that the level of evil can trigger a divine determination to terminate as a last resort to stop wider destruction? We have so emphasized the Priestly love of God in today's church that it is almost unthinkable that God would hate those advancing evil enough to terminate them. But we must remember *"Love never fails..."* means that God hates what destroys His people. By only preaching what we like, we neglect the judicial passages. But no one can re-translate Revelation 2:14-16 to make it mean anything else. It says, *"But I have a few things against you, because you have there those who hold the doctrine of Balaam, who taught Balak to put a stumbling block before the children of Israel, to eat things sacrificed to idols, and to commit sexual immorality. Thus you also have those who hold the doctrine of the Nicolaitans, which thing I hate. Repent, or else I will come to you quickly and will fight against them with the sword of My mouth."* Jesus says He loves His people enough that when the doctrine of the Nicolaitans is welcomed in a church, He hates it to the point that He will come and fight against those people with the Sword of His mouth. When Jesus releases the Sword of His mouth, I suspect termination will come into play. What is the doctrine of the Nicolaitans? It is the belief that the primary essence of a man is spirit – so whatever we do with our bodies does not make a difference.[v] In this doctrine, sexual sin is not an issue because there is grace for everything. In Revelation 2, this attitude brought the Warrior Jesus on the scene. If today's church is slipping into that doctrine, we trust Warrior Jesus will not hesitate to respond to judicial prayers.

Revelation 2:20-23 says, *"Nevertheless I have a few things against you, because you allow that woman Jezebel, who calls herself a prophetess, to teach and seduce My servants to commit sexual immorality and eat things sacrificed to idols. And I gave her time to repent of her sexual immorality, and she did not repent. Indeed I will cast her into a sickbed, and those who commit adultery with her into great tribulation, unless they repent of their deeds. I will kill her children with death, and all the churches shall know that I am He who searches the minds and hearts. And I will give to each one of you according to your works."* Jesus promised to terminate the proponents of false doctrine in the second generation. Love will intervene to terminate before sin can destroy a generation. Do we have a generation that is being utterly destroyed by thinking sexual immorality is OK? We absolutely do. What should we expect Heaven's loving response to be? According to Revelation 2, there is termination coming. I expect Layer Five of God's love will be released in the land, in order to save. God is love and love never fails. So the divine response to evil that may be required to save our nation will be love that terminates! When Terminator Jesus visits, He will go to the church first! Until then, we may experience catastrophic events that hurt everyone. Sadly, the innocent at times perish with the guilty. Catastrophic events are increasing as iniquity increases in nations. How many more catastrophic events do you suppose will come to nations before the church begins to activate God's Loving Hand to terminate those responsible for taking our nation down the path of destruction? Love terminates in order to save. And our Bible tells us that love never fails. What does that mean for each Christian? What does that mean for the prayer life of each believer? When nations are faced with ruthless political leaders, what does it mean that love never fails? What did *"Love never fails..."* mean to Dietrich Bonhoeffer when Hitler was in power? Bonhoeffer preached against the cheap grace that allowed Hitler to take power in Germany.

What is cheap grace allowing today? Do we have Hitlers in power already? How did Bonhoeffer respond to evil as a Christian leader? Bonhoeffer took action and confronted the evil. Let our action follow the Davidic model by praying God's Hand on the perpetrators. Psalm 143:12 is what David prayed on those who took Jerusalem with Absalom, *"In Your mercy cut off my enemies, and destroy all those who afflict my soul, For I am your servant."* God answered David's prayers and let us expect Him to answer ours!

Psalm 97:1-9 states, *"The Lord reigns; Let the earth rejoice; Let the multitude of isles be glad! Clouds and darkness surround Him Righteousness and justice are the foundation of His Throne. A fire goes before Him, And burns up His enemies round about. His lightnings light the world; The earth sees and trembles. The mountains melt like wax at the presence of the Lord, At the presence of the Lord of the whole earth. The heavens declare His righteousness, And all the peoples see His glory. Let all be put to shame who serve carved images Who boast of idols. Worship Him, all you gods. Zion hears and is glad, And the daughters of Judah rejoice Because of Your judgments, O Lord. For You, Lord, are most high above all the earth; You are exalted far above all gods."* This passage portrays God as a God who sets righteousness and justice as the foundation of His Throne. The Scripture speaks of fire that goes before Him to terminate those who choose to be His enemies. Verse 6 says, *"The heavens declare His righteousness, And all the peoples see His glory."* Verse 7 says, *"Let all be put to shame who serve carved images, Who boast of idols. Worship Him, all you gods."* Verse 8 says, *"Zion hears and is glad, And the daughters of Judah rejoice Because of Your judgments, O Lord."* Verse 9 says, *"For You, Lord, are most high above all the earth; You are exalted far above all gods."* In verse 10, we are plainly commanded to hate evil. This passage says, *"You who love the Lord, hate evil! He preserves the souls of His saints; He delivers them out of the hand of the wicked."* Probably one of the toughest things for today's believers is to consider that we are to hate evil. We have been so inundated with the kindness emphasis of God's love, that it is inconceivable that we should hate anything. Some in the church vote for evil-doers and support them. Many in this nation condemn gun violence against children but support abortion-on-demand. No nation can condone murdering the children they do not want and then protect the children they do want! Abortion has spiritual consequences. Jesus hates the evil that destroys His creation. And we are told to have the same attitude! Do we hate evil enough to pray termination on those who refuse to turn from it? Until the church shoulders its responsibility, how can we expect a harvest of nations?

Proverbs 8:12-16 states, *"I, wisdom, dwell with prudence, And find out knowledge and discretion. The fear of the Lord is to hate evil; Pride and arrogance and the evil way And the perverse mouth I hate. Counsel is mine, and sound wisdom; I am understanding, I have strength. By me kings reign, And rulers decree justice. By me princes rule, and nobles, All the judges of the earth."* Wisdom is the key to knowledge and that truth has its foundation in the fear of the Lord. But the way to tell if we fear the Lord is whether we hate what God hates. If we do not hate evil, arrogance, the lying mouth and the evil way, then we are passing over the very foundation of wisdom and knowledge that give us biblical application by the Holy Spirit. This passage even proclaims that by these things, kings reign and rulers decree justice. Jesus made us Kings and Priests. Therefore, these are the rules by which we must operate if we are going to step into that Kingly ministry. Proverbs goes on to say in verse 17, *"I love those who love me, And those who seek me diligently will find me."* How can we ignore that the fear of the Lord hates evil? It is a cornerstone of being a King and moving in the Holy Spirit.

Isaiah had to prophesy judgment because of the continuing rebellion of Israel. Isaiah 9:15 says, *"For the people do not turn to Him who strikes them, Nor do they seek the Lord of hosts. Therefore the Lord will cut off head and tail from Israel, Palm branch and bulrush in one day. The elder and honorable, he is the head; The prophet who teaches lies, he is the tail. For the leaders of this people cause them to err, And those who are led by them are destroyed."* God hates evil to the point that when it fills the cup of iniquity, He moves in order to save the very creation which cries out against the iniquity of the inhabitants of the land. The land can only hold so much iniquity. The way to save a nation is the way Moses did on four different occasions. He prayed the perpetrators into judgment in order to save the nation itself. Is that possible for us? Do we have enough believers who have cultivated a hatred of evil that matches God's? Are there enough believers acquainted with their Kingly role to pray judgment on evil-doers until they see it happen? If not, we can grow to that place!

Amos 5:14,15 says, *"Seek good and not evil, That you may live; So the Lord God of hosts will be with you, As you have spoken. Hate evil, love good; Establish justice in the gate. It may be that the Lord God of hosts Will be gracious to the remnant of Joseph."* Amos had a message for his generation and that message was very strong. The message was also simple – hate what God hates and love what God loves. From that foundation you can establish justice in the gate. Justice in the gate seems to be the fruit of a people who agree with God and pray accordingly. When we pray for removal or termination of those who fill a land with iniquity, we are actually praying to save the remainder of the nation or remnant, and to ultimately save the land. That is the love of God in action! Love terminates in order to save.

Psalm 15:1-4 says,

Lord, who may abide in Your tabernacle? Who may dwell in Your holy hill? He who walks uprightly, And works righteousness, And speaks the truth in his heart; He who does not backbite with his tongue, Nor does evil to his neighbor, Nor does he take up a reproach against his friend; In whose eyes a vile person is despised, But he honors those who fear the Lord; He who swears to his own hurt and does not change;...

Psalm 15 is crucial. It is a foundational understanding for any of us who want to walk in intimacy and maturity with the Lord. That is obvious from the way it begins, *"Lord, who may abide in Your tabernacle? Who may dwell in Your holy hill?"* If we are going to spend time with the Lord, there are certain attitudes that He requires. He demands that in our eyes, *"a vile person is despised."* We have had so much indoctrination in what the church calls the "love of God," that we do not despise anyone. Instead we 'love' everyone. It is a good thing to love everyone so we can offer them salvation. But the real question is, do we despise evil actions that not only bring individual captivity but ultimately will destroy the land? Is it possible to do what this verse says? This verse says, it is difficult to separate a person from their actions when they consistently, arrogantly embrace and trumpet those actions. In order to discover what actions will ultimately destroy a land, we must find what Scripture says is vile. If Scripture does not say it is vile, it is not on the list. But if Scripture says it is vile, it is enough to threaten a land and it is enough to warrant prayers for termination. What does God consider vile enough to have to despise those who publicly promote the activity? This does not mean we despise those who are ashamed of and hide their activities. This is talking about those who publicly support or promote the vile activity. We have to ask ourselves, do we despise any vile behaviors or vile individuals? Do we despise any persons because of their biblically condemned behavior? Most Christians that I know, do not! Most do not despise anyone at all.

And yet, if we are going to dwell on God's Holy Hill, **vile people must be despised**! I wonder what behaviors and the public promotion of them, qualifies for this list?

In Judges 19:22-20:5, the men of Gibeah demanded that a certain resident bring out the traveler that had just come into the city because they wanted to "know him." Verse 24 says, *"Look, here is my virgin daughter and the man's concubine; let me bring them out now. Humble them, and do with them as you please; but to this man do not do such a vile thing!"* Certain sexual sin qualifies as a vile thing. The man of the house refused the request. They brought out the concubine, and she was abused all night and consequently killed.

The Levite took his concubine back to his place, dismembered her, piece-by-piece, and sent a piece to every one of the tribes of Israel. They came together and God ordered them to attack Gibeah. God sets certain sin and the promotion of it apart as vile. But there is a distinct difference between people who are caught in the sin and those who publicly, blatantly and actively promote it. God was willing to decimate the tribe of Benjamin in order to remove what the Bible defined as vile behavior. What should we be praying over our politicians who are protecting and promoting sexual sin? If we truly want to reside on God's Holy Hill and continue to have a relationship with Him, how should we pray over senators, representatives, judges and even presidents? Psalm 110 tells us what God is willing to do! Psalm 110 states,

> *The Lord said to my Lord, "Sit at My right hand, Till I make Your enemies Your footstool." The Lord shall send the rod of Your strength out of Zion. Rule in the midst of Your enemies! Your people shall be volunteers In the day of Your power; In the beauties of holiness, from the womb of the morning, You have*

the dew of Your youth. The Lord has sworn And will not relent, "You are a priest forever According to the order of Melchizedek." The Lord is at Your right hand; He shall execute kings in the day of His wrath. He shall judge among the nations, He shall fill the places with dead bodies, He shall execute the heads of many countries. He shall drink of the brook by the wayside; Therefore He shall lift up the head.

Every believer should memorize Psalm 110 because God's interventions proclaimed herein are needed in the last days!

Psalm 12:1-8 is another passage declaring God's response to evil,

Help, Lord, for the godly man ceases! For the faithful disappear from among the sons of men. They speak idly everyone with his neighbor; With flattering lips and a double heart they speak. May the Lord cut off all flattering lips, And the tongue that speaks proud things, Who have said, "With our tongue we will prevail; Our lips are our own; Who is lord over us?" "For the oppression of the poor, for the sighing of the needy, Now I will arise," says the Lord; "I will set him in the safety for which he yearns." The words of the Lord are pure words, Like silver tried in a furnace of earth, Purified seven times. You shall keep them, O Lord, You shall preserve them from this generation forever. The wicked prowl on every side, When vileness is exalted among the sons of men.

Are the wicked prowling on every side? When there is no judgment on what is considered vile by God, wickedness begins to accelerate throughout the culture. The fastest way to bring destruction on a nation is to promote what God considers vile. When there is no longer penalty for vile actions and leaders begin to promote what God considers vile, you will have an explosion of evil and wickedness in a society. It appears as if we are there. Either the church must stand up and bring the Hand of God against the perpetrators or we will start losing cities. *"Love never fails"* means termination can be prayed to save cities and ultimately nations! Will the church dwell in God's Holy Hill?

I have a friend active in community affairs who related this story to me. A mother came searching for her daughter who was out of school and working at her first job. The mother was concerned as there was no contact for several months. The police went with the mother to the daughter's home. The daughter was not there and the locks had been changed. The home was still rented in her daughter's name, but the current occupants denied knowledge of her daughter. The police traced the occupants to a prostitution ring in a large city. It turned out a woman had befriended her, drugged her and smuggled her out of her home state and into sexual slavery. How could this happen to a young working girl in a safe neighborhood? The police said it happens all the time! If there ever was a group worthy of justice, it is every contributor to sex trafficking: both the traffickers, and the customers who create the demand!

Romans 12:1 says, *"I beseech you therefore, brethren, by the mercies of God, that you present your bodies a living sacrifice, holy, acceptable to God, which is your reasonable service."* When we present our bodies as a living sacrifice, holy and acceptable to God, then we are agreeing to do what He has called us to do – regardless of what the price is, in the nation or society in which we live. In Romans 12, this call precedes a section in verses 3-21 that in the New King James Study Bible is entitled *"Responsibilities toward Society."* God says if we are going to walk with Him in the last days, we are going to be His agents of justice. And that justice comes by prayer, proclamation and declaration. God's termination of Ananias and Sapphira came by Peter's words. The ultimate impact of the prayers uttered by the church when Peter was in jail culminated in moving Herod toward termination. The tipping point of Herod's execution was his accepting worship. God saved Peter and blindness was released on the false prophet by Paul's words. In the days ahead, the church has the responsibility of bringing in an end-time harvest. Is there any doubt that the only way to do that is to move the Hand of God on those who are hindering it? It will take an ultimate commitment to God in order to be willing to go there. Are we willing? Our culture does not currently despise vileness, but God ***does***. And if we are going to reside on His Holy Hill, we have to also. Previous generations despised those who chose vile behaviors! I believe the Word draws a distinction between those who publicly promote a behavior and those who are caught in the sin of it. The public promoters are the ones Scripture denounces as worthy of death! I believe a great harvest will come out of groups enslaved by sin! The Priestly side of Christ extends mercy and grace to all who are caught in the deception of the sin. As agents of Christ, we depend on the Holy Spirit to lead us to present Priestly salvation or Kingly justice!

Romans 1:24-26 states, *"Therefore God also gave them up to uncleanness, in the lusts of their hearts, to dishonor their bodies among themselves, who exchanged the truth of God for the lie, and worshiped and served the creature rather than the Creator, who is blessed forever. Amen. For this reason God gave them up to vile passions. For even their women exchanged the natural use for what is against nature."* The same actions that the Old Testament called vile are also vile in the New Testament. Jesus Christ is the same yesterday, today and forever. What He deems vile remains vile today. What God demands we despise as vile in order to dwell in His Holy Hill is called vile in the New Testament also. We should ask ourselves if the penalty is the same in the New Testament as it was in the Old? If that is the case, then the love of God is a two-edged sword. One edge offers salvation to those caught in deception, but the second edge brings a cutting off of those who blatantly and boldly revel in their sin. Can we go there with Jesus in prayer? Can we separate the sinner from their sin on a Priestly mission while praying termination on a Kingly assignment?

Romans 1:27-32 states, *"Likewise also the men, leaving the natural use of the woman, burned in their lust for one another, men with men committing what is shameful, and receiving in themselves the penalty of their error which was due. And even as they did not like to retain God in their knowledge, God gave them over to a debased mind, to do those things which are not fitting; being filled with all unrighteousness, sexual immorality, wickedness, covetousness, maliciousness; full of envy, murder, strife, deceit, evil-mindedness; they are whisperers, backbiters, haters of God, violent, proud, boasters, inventors of evil things, disobedient to parents, undiscerning, untrustworthy, unloving, unforgiving, unmerciful; who, knowing the righteous judgment of God, that those who practice such things are deserving of death, not only do the same but also approve of those who practice them."* These are heart-wrenching verses when our children are caught in the deception. Praying the Sword to separate ungodly relationships is a very Kingly option. It is obvious that the very same penalty for vile behavior in the Old Testament is the same in the New. What is our attitude toward people who publicly promote vile behaviors? If there is a refusal to repent, we should consistently be praying and declaring God's termination! Those who are caught in the deception of the behavior should get the other side, the Priestly offer of salvation. But when that offer is consistently rejected to the point of public promotion, our response has to change. God does the terminating, but our job is to do the praying!

Just like love terminated the vile in Noah's day, Noah himself found grace. The love that Noah found saved him and his family in the midst of global termination. That is a picture for every believer and their family today. Regardless of what our kids or grandkids are caught up in, the promise is that we can find grace by standing in the gap. Our prayers and intercession bring salvation to our family members. The love of Jesus never fails and His love terminates in order to save. Can we walk with Him in this dimension in the last days to gain our promised harvest? I trust we can!

◆ Al Houghton ◆

Chapter 17

Love in its Fullness

Christians are called to be agents of both salvation and judgment. Love that fails to judge wickedness is an invention of man's mind. God's love gives righteous believers access to His judgment. Jesus completed the first segment of His dissertation on love in Matthew 5 by exhorting in verse 48, *"Therefore you shall be perfect just as your Father in heaven is perfect."* The English-speaking world with our cultural definition of perfect cannot embrace that statement. If *"perfect"* means having never made a mistake, we know we are doomed. Perfect, as we know it, is an ill-chosen translation for the concept of developmental growth into maturity or wholeness. **Tel-i-os** is the Greek word and it means to grow into maturity so that we can accomplish our destiny. Jesus had to grow into wisdom, favor and stature with God and man. He grew into His destiny. **Tel-i-os** means to grow into a place of maturity so that we can shoulder our destiny.

The Love Chapter, 1 Corinthians 13:9-13, exhorts us to grow into love,

> *For we know in part and we prophesy in part. But when that which is perfect has come, then that which is in part will be done away. When I was a child, I spoke as a child, I understood as a child, I thought as a child; but when I became a man, I put away childish things. For now we see in a mirror, dimly, but then face to face. Now I know in part, but then I shall know just as I also*

am known. And now abide faith, hope, love, these three; but the greatest of these is love.

We start our Christian walk with "turn-the-other-cheek" and "pray-for-the-enemy" love. But as we meet lethal adversaries, we are must grow into advanced applications of love!

I have a prophetic friend who, over the years, I have grown to really respect and very much appreciate for his accuracy. For many decades I have witnessed his choices in life and ministry, and to me his words carry a weightiness of a true man of God. Recently, this brother sent me his Holy Spirit imparted definition of mature Christian love:

> *"He who does not love does not know God, for God is love." 1 John 4:8*

> *The love I am speaking about in the Bible book of 1 John is Divine Love. Divine Love does not come from the unredeemed, it comes from My SPIRIT who resides in those people who are truly born by My SPIRIT and who are part of the Family of GOD.*

> *My true sons and daughters are trained by My SPIRIT to love what I love and to hate what I hate.*

> *My Love is a Spiritual Concept.*

> *Spiritual Qualities cannot be discerned or defined by the human soul, containing the intellect, the emotions, the will and the personality of humans.*

Ask Me to reveal to you all the misconceptions you have about My Love, so you are better able to walk in the Way of Understanding that leads to My Life.

Many people do not understand My Love, and therefore the definition of My Love is misapplied. My Love cannot be defined in human terms. For example to say I love what is evil is a misrepresentation of My Divine Character.

Ask Me, the SPIRIT OF TRUTH, to define the Love of GOD. Allow Me to teach you, a sincere seeker of My Truth, about My Love.

Ask Me to teach you about many deceptions being taught falsely about My Love in contemporary "Christian" circles.

My Love is epitomized by the Gifts of My SON, My Word, and My SPIRIT. Those who hate My SON, My Word and My SPIRIT are outside of My Love.

I love righteousness.

I love justice.

I do not love what profanes My Name and destroys My people.

My Love selects and safeguards a people who will wear My Name with honor and who will do what I ask of them.

My Love is refining a people who are willing to bear My Name. All those who refuse to embrace My Refining Fires are outside of My Love.

My Love compels Me to go to war. I war against all that is evil and unrighteous.

My Love always labors to destroy the works of the Devil and the Kingdom of Darkness.

People claim they can sin all they want and remain in My Love, because they say I am obligated to love them unconditionally. This is not true.

My Love has many conditions: the first and foremost is obedience to receive the Gifts of My Grace and My Creation; to be the person I created you to be.

My Love requires that My SON, JESUS CHRIST, be honored. Those who despise My SON are outside of My Love. Those who are outside of My Love are outside of My Life and outside of My Light of Truth.

My Love requires a submission to My Divine Laws and Divine Order. You cannot say I love the lawless, the disrespectful, the ungrateful, and the destroyers of what is good, righteous, and just. I fight against many people. I put My enemies under My Feet. If I am fighting against people, or putting an enemy of Mine under My Feet, how am I covering them with My Love?

People say that I must forgive, because I am the GOD OF LOVE. I do not forgive the unrepentant. I do not forgive those who willfully do evil. I do not forgive those who refuse to be honest with Me and with others their dishonesty hurts.

I do not love haters of truth. It is a lie to say that the HOLY GOD, the GOD whose Name is LOVE loves everybody; that everyone is covered by My Love, and that I must extend My Grace to everyone because I am obligated to love them.

My Love is completely focused. I give My Grace to repent, but when there is no repentance, and there is a continuing willful demonstration of evil and unrighteous behaviors, then My Love decides to cut these souls off from the Light of My Life.

My Love sets the boundaries to evil and to evil behavior.

My Love terminates the lives of wicked people around the earth every day.

My Love will destroy this earth and all the wickedness done in this earth.

My Love will ultimately create a New Heavens and a New Earth where Righteousness will dwell Forever.

My Love removes what defiles.

  My Love disciplines and corrects.

My Love never enables evil.

This is not the humanistic view of the "love of God".

My Love is Holy.

My Love is Just.

My Love is Pure.

I mean what I say, and I say what I mean. My Love always speaks the Truth. My Love champions the Truth.

My Love is not manipulated.

My Love is based on covenant. Those who refuse to abide by My Terms of Covenant are outside of My Love.

My Love creates and destroys.

My Love does not tolerate the destruction of My precious children. Those who destroy My children will receive the full extent of My Wrath. My Wrath is an expression of My Love.

My Love judges with Holy Fire.

My Love hates spiritual and natural adultery.

My Love hates when families are destroyed by the willful evil of a parent. My Love hates those who willfully take advantage of others.

My Love rescues, comforts, heals and delivers and also, judges, removes, separates and destroys.

The statement, "It is a fearful thing to fall into the hands of the LIVING GOD." (Hebrews 10:31), is a definition of the fierceness of My Love.

My Love protects and provides for those who are Mine.

My Love cuts off those who delight to do the Devil's work.

My Love is defined by all that I AM – My Righteousness, My Holiness, My Mercy and My Justice.

My Love is Kind and Severe.

My Love is an All Consuming Fire.

Those who embrace My Love will be able to stand in the Fire of My HOLY PRESENCE.

Those who reject and despise My Love will be consumed by My Holy Fire.

My Love never fails.

Human love can easily fail.

What is Eternal is Eternal and what is temporal is temporal.

Human love is temporal.

My Love is Eternal.

Seeker of Truth, ask Me to reveal to you the Height, Depth, Breadth and Width of My Love. Do this and you will discover the Fullness of My Life."[vi]

Tel-i-os leads us to all the other layers of God's love in the New Testament. If we are to be growing into God's image then we must love the way God loves in any given situation. In Acts and Revelation, God loves the church enough to remove those hindering our harvest who refuse to repent. The book of Revelation is essential in preparing the church today for walking with Jesus to possess an end-time harvest!

1 John probably defines God's love best in the New Testament and **tel-i-os** is an integral part of what is taught as a growth pattern. In 1 John 1:5-7, John stresses the relational aspect of love by declaring,

> *This is the message which we have heard from Him and declare to you, that God is light and in Him is no darkness at all. If we say that we have fellowship with Him, and walk in darkness, we lie and do not practice the truth. But if we walk in the light as He is in the light, we have fellowship with one another, and the blood of Jesus Christ His Son cleanses us from all sin.*

It is through fellowship and relationship that our dysfunctions emerge so that they can be dealt with. It is through fellowship that we hold each other accountable. It is through fellowship that the love of God grows into maturity. John makes this foundationally clear. In 1 John 2:3-6 we are told, *"Now by this we know that we know Him, if we keep His commandments. He who says, 'I know Him,' and does not keep His commandments, is a liar, and the truth is not in him. But whoever keeps His word, truly the love of God is **perfected** in him. By this we know that we are in Him. He who says he abides in Him ought himself also to walk just as He walked."* The Greek word **tel-i-os** appears in verse 5. If we incorporate the truth of God's Word, if we bridle our body and our mind and begin to conform it to Scripture, if we integrate the Word into our lives, then, John says, the love of God is matured in us. Verse 5 says, *"...the love of God is perfected..."* or *has been matured*, so it governs our thinking. Being a doer of God's Word is emulating who

Jesus is in both the Gospels and Revelation. What accounts for Jesus' different responses from raising the dead, to making them dead? Jesus raised a widow's dead son at Nain. Jesus killed Ananias and Sapphira. If we mature in love, we will experience both dimensions by the Spirit. If we only accept one response for love – the passive, "turn-the-other-cheek," accepting response – then we have fallen into a passive tradition and the Lord has doubts about us and, according to Paul, he would like to cut off the people responsible for taking the spiritual manhood from the church. Galatians 5:9-13 states,

> *A little leaven leavens the whole lump. I have confidence in you, in the Lord, that you will have no other mind; but he who troubles you shall bear his judgment, whoever he is. And I, brethren, if I still preach circumcision, why do I still suffer persecution? Then the offense of the cross has ceased. I could wish that those who trouble you would even cut themselves off! For you, brethren, have been called to liberty; only do not use liberty as an opportunity for the flesh, but through love serve one another.*

A church in passivity has been spiritually castrated. It is obvious that John understood the love of God. As long as the enemy can convince the church that love only means "turn-the-other-cheek" and pray for the enemy, we have a passive church enabling evil! The most destructive traditions have a clear scriptural foundation where only one aspect of an issue is emphasized while all the others are excluded. This kind of limited love has become a devastating tradition making a passive, ineffective church when confronting evil whether in religion, government or culture!

1 John 4:7-9 says, *"Beloved, let us love one another, for love is of God; and everyone who loves is born of God and knows God. He who does not love does not know God, for God is love. In this the love of God*

was manifested toward us, that God has sent His only begotten Son into the world, that we might live through Him." Herod killed James and jailed Peter, expecting to kill him also. Peter was scheduled for death. The love of God to save Peter had no other choice but to destroy Herod. *Love never fails!!* When does love have to destroy in order to save? Whenever our destiny or harvest field is threatened, covenant love is obligated to intervene! James fulfilled his call by joining the martyrs.

The love of God is defined for us by John, through this passage. It reveals the Incarnate Christ. Why have we chosen to discount the judicial actions of Christ as if they were not there? The first component for growth is we choose to be doers of the Word. As we conform our thoughts and actions to God's Word, we are matured in love. He tells us again that loving one another *is* incorporating God's Word into our lives. Verses 10-12 state, *"In this is love, not that we loved God, but that He loved us and sent His Son to be the propitiation for our sins. Beloved, if God so loved us, we also ought to love one another. No one has seen God at any time. If we love one another, God abides in us, and His love has been perfected/tel-i-os, matured, in us."*

Verse 12 makes it clear that, in John's understanding, growing in the Word is growing in love. Growing in love means maturing in our responses until we can mirror the full spectrum of God's responses to man. The limited, kindness-only definition of love results in us being enablers of evil. This is the furthest thing from John's view of maturity. Love, in John's definition, can *pull* a person out of the grave or *put* a purveyor of wickedness in the grave. And it is God's choice, not ours. Jesus only did what He saw His Father doing. Jesus killed a fig tree then terrorized a religious system by overturning their tables and stripping them. His Own Hand made the weapon! Mature love looks just like Jesus. Matthew 15:13 states, *"...Every plant which My heavenly Father has not planted will be uprooted."* How many licentious leaders and mammonite politicians have we uprooted in prayer? God may not let us overturn mammonite politicians until we see mammonite ministers overturned! Be aware that termination can mean the cutting off of job, office, position or life. Judgment begins at the house of God. Mature love is coming to the church and it is not turning the other cheek! When God exposes sin, the light shines on the darkness, and God is visiting the church!

1 John 4:15,16 states, "...*Whoever confesses that Jesus is the Son of God, God abides in him, and he in God. And we have known and believed the love that God has for us. God is love, and he who abides in love abides in God, and God in him.*" John declared that God *is* love. We understand that *everything* God does is a manifestation of love. It is not just that God loves, but that He fully and completely **is** love! When Jesus cleaned house in the temple, He was manifesting a measure of God's love. When Jesus confronted the demon-possessed man and delivered him, He was manifesting a measure of God's love. The early church witnessed the love that killed Ananias and Sapphira? What have we witnessed?

The Spirit moved dramatically to purify the early church of the love of money! If the Lord allowed Ananias and Sapphira to go unchecked, they would have defiled many with their compromised spirit. He stopped the defilement before the transition brought by the persecution of Stephen, otherwise each new church would have carried a mammon-seed. Jesus guaranteed the purity of each church-plant! Today's passive church might turn the other cheek and pray blessing on Ananias and Sapphira. But if the early church had walked as today's church, they would have had many compromised outposts! How often do we work against God in the name of love? Has our doctrine made us nicer than God? The apostles saw Jesus move in both love that saves *and* love that kills! They imitated Jesus. Are *we* really imitating the New Testament Christ?

1 John 4:17 says, *"Love has been perfected among us in this: that we may have boldness in the day of judgment; because as He is, so are we in this world."* Why is the enemy working hard to insure that most of the church will never experience this truth? Love has been matured among us when we have boldness in the Day of Judgment because as He is, so are we in this world. How is Jesus conducting Himself and moving His purpose forward right now? When is the Day of Judgment? When was the Day of Judgment for Ananias and Sapphira? When was the Day of Judgment for Herod? When did Peter need a Day of Judgment to be saved? Was the Day of Judgment the day Peter needed God's judgment to finish his race?

Oh that, *"...as He is, so are we..."* would become real to the church! Jesus is seated at the right Hand of God. He is the Judge of all the Earth. He is capable of rendering a judicial decision in our behalf against congressmen, senators, governors or presidents. He is capable of blinding an enemy and He is capable of terminating any enemy of the harvest!

If *"...as He is, so are we..."* is true, then we have access to the Judge of all the Earth any place, anytime and anywhere. Is that the reason that the very next verse, 1 John 4:18, says, *"There is no fear in love; but perfect love casts out fear, because fear involves torment. But he who fears has not been made perfect/**tel-i-oo** in love."* Does the church walk in that place? Is the church fearless?

I can understand how we could be fearless if verse 17 became a working, living reality to us! It would mean that we have ongoing, daily access to the judgment of God anywhere and anytime. There would be no fear in us because we would be matured in all the layers of God's love and we could stand in the fire we would have to call down. How much of our destiny are we forfeiting individually, corporately and nationally, because we operate only in Priestly love? But if we get to know the Jesus who has different displays of His love not only in the Old Testament but also in our New Testament, then we can understand how to walk without fear, because as He is, so are we in this world.

John, the man who wrote the book of Revelation, stood against an emperor and was only exiled when multiple attempts to kill him failed, they even tried to boil him in oil. He simply would not boil. John, the Revelator, believed and lived, "...*as He is, so are we in this world.*" It is always better to write about what you have experienced. The emperor could not kill him. All he could do was exile John to a place where he wrote the book of Revelation as a fearless representative of the Lord Jesus Christ. Our destiny is to fully model Jesus. John was very close. And he said that the key was love. It is time we embraced and agreed to walk in each layer of God's love so that we may possess the great end-time harvest!

I am convinced that each of the five-fold ministries are endowed with a Layer of God's love that naturally flows from their piece of God's Heart! Each ministry gift has the responsibility of duplicating the piece of God's Heart that has been imparted to them. They are to impart it to the body and grow the church into representing that piece of God's Heart. But each of the five-fold has a very different piece to impart. The evangelistic piece is very, very different from the prophetic piece. The differences in how love is applied are more varied than the range of the color kaleidoscope. The evangelist first and foremost loves the sinner. The prophet first and foremost loves purity. In identical situations, their response to individuals is utterly and totally different than other members of the five-fold. An evangelist compassionately loves the lost into truth through his ability to overlook evil. At times, evangelists seem to be oblivious to sin. They have been given an expression of love for the lost that is unconditional acceptance. That love can be so great they tend to completely overlook sin and in kindness love a person into the Kingdom. The evangelist is empowered to turn the other cheek and pray for his enemies. When in the evangelistic mode we do not resist an evil person, but that is the only time. Jesus dramatically resisted evil when moving as a prophet. As the resurrected Apostle and High Priest of our profession, He judges evil.

An evangelist defaults to turning the other cheek but a prophet is wired differently. A prophet has an entirely different heart. What he is wired to focus on is how 'radical surgery' could likely save the individual from the 'cancer' of the world that is eating that person's life into oblivion. So the prophet will nearly always pull out a dull knife and begin the surgery, assuming that whatever pain he causes will help as an instrument towards growth in a friend as well as in a land. Prophets tend to think, the more pain, the less likelihood of returning to the sin and wallowing in the mire. Prophets have a heart to purify and they sometimes seem insulated to the pain of the people in the process. Prophets, like Jesus, weave cords into whips and overturn tables and drive out injustice. Because the giftings of evangelists and pastors are emphasized most in the church, the fruit of "turn-the-other-cheek" and forbearance are most highly developed in the body. As persecution increases, the need for the prophet's warning, the teacher's affliction and apostolic termination will rise as we move deeper into the end-times. The church will only be ready for persecution when all the Layers of God's love are developed! The church has a highly developed sense of Jesus the Savior, but needs to equally develop the sense of Jesus the Judge!

Every ministry gift has its own unique piece of God's Heart and the bearer is responsible for duplicating, *strengthening* and reinforcing their piece in the lives of all to whom they minister. The five-fold ministry represents five layers of God's love and each one has its own unique purpose, its own unique message and its own unique application. If we want to mature in the love of God, we need to allow representatives of each one of these ministry gifts to impart their heart to us. Then and only then will we achieve the fearlessness and preparation that God intends the church to have in the last days.

We need to understand that the same love displayed to Abraham in his covenant is covenant love that is duplicated in the Mosaic, Deuteronomic, Davidic and New Covenants. Love has a judicial application. Jesus truly has not changed and is the same yesterday, today and forever! Covenant love saves and covenant love through prayer moves God's Hand to remove promoters of evil. Blessed be the name of the Lord! Can we move in the fullness of that love? God's Hand moving to cut off the enemies of our harvest field should parallel God's Hand moving for David. He prayed and God destroyed his enemies. If God loved us enough to send Jesus to die to save us, does He not love us enough to kill to preserve us? Faith to challenge evil arises from knowing Jesus the Judge. It is time for us to get to know Him.

◆ Al Houghton ◆

Endnotes

[i] Weymouth, Richard Francis. Hampden–Cook, Ernest. Ed. *The New Testament in Modern Speech*, 3rd Ed. Boston, Pilgrim Press. 1911. Print.

[ii] Kittel, Gerhard, Ed. Theological Dictionary of the New Testament, V. 1. Grand Rapids, WM,B. Eerdmans Publishing Co. 1964. 407 p. Print.

[iii] Ham, Edward E. *50 Years on the Battle Front with Christ: A Biography of Mordecai F. Ham*. Old Kentucky Home Revivalist, 1950. 32 p. Print.

[iv] Rushdooney, Rousas John. *The Foundations of Social Order*. Phillipsburg, Presbyterian & Reformed Publishing Company, 1978. 17 p. Print.

[v] Vincent's Word Studies in the New Testament 4 volumes,. 1887, Marvin R. Vincent Logos Bible Software, 2720 p 2002. Charles Scribner's & Sons, 1887-1995. EPrint.

[vi] Received as a Gift of the Spirit, a word of wisdom, (1 Corinthians 12:8a) by Kingdom Ministries; 2013.

About the Author

Al Houghton is a Father in the Faith formed in the fire. He is a proven prophetic voice who tempers his words by the yardstick of Scripture. Approximately forty years of ministry now include over thirty-three years of Word At Work daily Bible studies, six books & a library of CD and MP3 teaching series that form the foundation for leaders on all seven continents.

In 1975, Al moved to California to attend seminary, obtained a Masters in Divinity degree, and there met and married his wife, Jayne. They began a teaching ministry which moved from home Bible studies to facilities like Mott Auditorium in Pasadena, CA, where he pastored for a decade. Al and Jayne have three children, Jonathan, Julie and Michael.

Jayne has a strong teaching gift and Julie a strong prophetic gift, making their input invaluable in collaboration in the Bible studies and books.

The Houghton's primary assignment is elevating the church into their Kingly Priesthood as "agents of justice." Acts 2:36 says, *"Therefore let all the house of Israel know assuredly that God has made this Jesus, whom you crucified both Lord* (**koo-ree-os**) *and Christ* (**khris-tos**)." Many believers only know the Priestly CHRIST, but do not know the Judicial LORD. As a result, most believers can "turn-the-other-cheek" but few can swing our Biblical, Judicial Sword.

Jesus manifested judicially when Al was first called into ministry. Ten years later, He began participating with the Judicial Christ and through the years has innumerable testimonies of Christ in action from warning to affliction to termination. Al's spiritual sons and daughters are proving the reality of the Judicial Christ among the nations.

JESUS & JUSTICE

Jesus paid the price for the church to function as "Kings and Priests." Jesus & Justice traces the development of the function of the priestly and kingly ministries. The primary passion of a priest was atonement or salvation, but kings had a very different assignment. Their God-given job was to judge and make war. Jesus in the gospels is the suffering servant priest who "turns the other cheek" to save. But when He ascended and took a seat at the right hand of God, He quickly became the King of Kings, Lord of Lords and Judge of all the Earth.

Jesus & Justice restores to the church the authority of the resurrected King. The absence of the fear of God proves biblical justice has morphed into social justice. Christians represent the Jesus of Revelation and have an obligation to move God's hand against evil when it manifests in their presence!

The early church walked in this demonstration of justice from praying Peter out of jail to praying the political leader Herod into judgment. Paul accessed this judicial realm when a false prophet captured a Proconsul, but blindness on the false prophet persuaded the politician. ***Jesus & Justice* releases this level of authority in the church while outlining the preparational path necessary to stand in the fire you have to call down! Imagine what the Judicial Christ can do restoring what has been stolen!**

THE SURE MERCIES OF DAVID

How should believers respond to the avalanche of evil assaulting our nation, cursing our biblical culture and outlawing the voices of virtue?

God covenanted with David to redeem his failure and cut off his enemies. David knew what to ask for to save his land, based on this covenant. Jesus guaranteed the covenant of "Sure Mercy" and Paul preached it in Acts 13 with a warning that failure to use it could cost the loss of cities, and even the nation.

"Sure Mercy" empowers the church by putting a two-edged sword in the hand of every believer. The first edge cuts away the guilt, shame and insecurity of personal failure allowing God to transform the failure into a foundation for future prophetic fulfillment. The second edge moves God's hand to execute biblical justice saving the nation from all those intent on perverting and destroying the land by filling it with iniquity!

Learning the difference between "Sure Mercy" for an individual and "Sure Mercy" for a nation empowers us to pray an entirely different way. David expressed in the Psalms God's heart for victory and His willingness to war in our behalf. This book helps the church war spiritually as David did physically!

MARKED MEN

God has promised end–time protections for His people as we navigate perilous times to accomplish a great end–time harvest. The prophetic tragedy of the last leadership generation is that they primarily equipped the church to recognize the mark of the counterfeit christ. The Bible promises nine real marks from the true Christ, each available for a specific end-time purpose. Almost every believer knows the counterfeit 666, but how many of us can name one of God's nine real marks enabling us to finish our call. Some of the questions answered are:

1. If we gain God's marks, are we protected from premature death till we finish our heavenly assignments? <u>The answer is, yes!</u>

2. Will Jesus come to the church before He comes for it, and if so, for what purpose? <u>Yes, He will. And the purpose will be judgment.</u>

3. If the cup has to be full before we can get a new heavens and earth, doesn't this make the pre-trib, mid and post arguments inconsequential? <u>No, but it does reduce their relevance.</u>

4. Are we preparing our children for the wrong rapture? How should we be training them for the future? <u>Yes – transition!</u>

5. How does the principle of fullness impact the church? Does fullness of iniquity demand fullness of Christ? <u>Bank on it!</u>

6. If in the end people must acquiesce to buy or sell, what must we do to achieve God's promised protection now? <u>Take God's marks.</u>

All materials available from our secure online store www.wordatwork.org or by calling us at 714-996-1015

PURIFYING THE ALTAR

The first consistent manifestations of the Judicial Christ developed as the Lord began unfolding a revelation concerning *Purifying The Altar*. The premier conflict of Scripture rages over our worship. Will we worship God or money? The issue dominated the disciples' relationship for three and one half years. At the last supper, they still could not discern the thief among them because there was "rivalry" over who should be the greatest! Whoever was in charge controlled the purse strings!

Purifying The Altar is a revolutionary and revelatory unfolding of the foundational principles that enable ever believer to stand on a Judicial platform with Christ declaring, decreeing and calling forth His Eternal Will! *Purifying The Altar* opens a whole new paradigm where we cooperate with the Holy Spirit in calling forth His Judicial plan. Isaiah 53:12 reveals that plan contains some radical manifestations, *"Therefore I will divide Him a portion with the great, And He shall divide the spoil with the strong, Because He poured out His soul unto death, And He was numbered with the transgressors, And He bore the sin of many, And made intercession for the transgressors."*

Jesus stated in Matthew 23, *"'Fools and blind! For which is greater, the gift or the altar that sanctifies the gift?'"* Jesus made the condition of the altar the determinant covenant factor. When an altar is cleansed so that it "sanctifies" what is given, the windows of heaven open because the covenant is actually consummated.

> *Purifying The Altar* is a study of the biblical principles which contribute to closing or opening the windows of heaven through purifying both the personal and corporate altars!

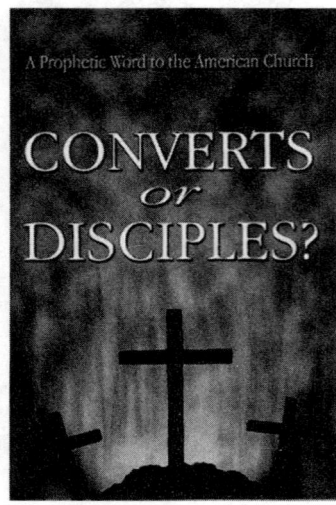

CONVERTS OR DISCIPLES?

Converts or Disciples is a prophetic word to the church, hopefully causing a reassessment of our ultimate purpose. If our number one goal is making disciples, then every believer we impact should be empowered to pass the 12 fold test of discipleship reflecting the commitment of the early church as they cultivated an apostolic culture!

1. True discipleship begins when we choose to embrace <u>Lordship</u>.
2. Converts walk where self wants, while disciples walk where <u>God wants.</u>
3. A convert sets his own <u>agenda</u>, while a disciple embraces God's <u>agenda</u>.
4. Converts often reject <u>God's plan</u>, while disciples accept it.
5. Converts use faith to <u>satisfy self</u>, while disciples use it to <u>satisfy God</u>.
6. Converts are oblivious to <u>manipulation</u> while disciples discern it.
7. Disciples volunteer for <u>hazardous duty</u>, while converts hesitate.
8. Disciples dare not covenant with <u>death</u> but converts do it repeatedly.
9. Disciples are vigilant about who their actions <u>worship</u>, but converts are not.
10. Disciples escape financial manipulation because they give by <u>revealed</u> need, while converts usually respond to <u>apparent</u> need.
11. Disciples display <u>Kingly Judicial Authority</u>, while converts do not.
12. Disciples have to extend <u>mercy</u>, while converts think it is optional.